MW00352638

Signing and Belonging in Nepal

Signing and Belonging in Nepal

Erika Hoffmann-Dilloway

Gallaudet University Press
Washington, DC

Gallaudet University Press
Washington, DC 20002
http://gupress.gallaudet.edu

Library of Congress Cataloging-in-Publication Data
Names: Hoffmann-Dilloway, Erika, author.
Title: Signing and belonging in Nepal / Erika Hoffmann-Dilloway.
Description: Washington, DC : Gallaudet University Press, [2016] | Includes
    bibliographical references and index.
Identifiers: LCCN 2015045471| ISBN 9781563686641 (hardcover : alk. paper) |
    ISBN 9781563686658 (e-book)
Subjects: LCSH: Deaf—Nepal. | Deaf—Means of communication—Nepal. | Sign
    language. | Anthropological linguistics.
Classification: LCC HV2855.9 .H64 2016 | DDC 305.9/082095496—dc23
LC record available at http://lccn.loc.gov/2015045471

Note: Some of the material in this book has appeared in previous publications. Parts of
chapter 3 appeared in a 2008 article titled "Metasemiotic Regimentation in the Standard-
ization of Nepali Sign Language" in the *Journal of Linguistic Anthropology* 18(2): 192–213.
Other sections of chapter 3 appeared in the 2010 article "Many Names for Mother: The
Ethno-Linguistic Politics of Deafness in Nepal," published in *South Asia: The Journal of
South Asian Studies* 33(3): 421–41. Parts of chapter 4 were published in 2011 as "Lending
a Hand: Competence through Cooperation in Nepal's Deaf Associations" in *Language in
Society* 40(3): 285–306. Finally, several elements of the 2011 article "Ordering Burgers,
Reordering Relations: Gestural Interactions between Hearing and d/Deaf Nepalis," which
was published in *Pragmatics* 21(3): 373–91, appear in chapter 5. I thank the publishers for
permission to reproduce this material here.

Cover photograph of Patan in Kathmandu, Nepal ©ziggymars/123RF.COM

Contents

Acknowledgments

MANY PEOPLE and institutions have helped to make this book possible. The Fulbright Institution of International Education/Commission for Educational Exchange between the United States and Nepal, the Foreign Language and Area Studies Fellowship Program of the U.S. Department of Education, and a Powers Travel Grant from Oberlin College provided funding.

My relationships in Nepal began when I was an undergraduate. I thank Peter Bertocci and Carlos Coppola from Oakland University for steering me in the right direction and both the School for International Training and the Kapali family for structuring my first experiences in Nepal. However, the bulk of this research was conducted while I was a graduate student at the University of Michigan from 2001 to 2008. There I received excellent training from Tom Fricke, Susan Gelman, Lakhan Gusain, Judith Irvine, Bruce Mannheim, Barbra Meek, Leslie Milroy, and others. I also received a great deal of support from my fellow graduate students, among whom I particularly thank Laura Brown, Nishaant Choksi, Sonia Das, Erica Pelta Feldman, Bridget Guarasci, Janak Rai, and Vanessa Will (several of whom also offered comments on drafts of this book). Additionally, I thank the members of the Michigan Anthropology Semiotics Reading Group, particularly Josh Reno, Cecilia Tomori, and Britt Halvorson, for their comments and for organizing a workshop that brought Rick Parmentier, whose observations on my project were extremely helpful, to visit our group.

I thank the Cornell Nepal Study Program (CNSP) in Kirtipur for allowing me to base my dissertation fieldwork from its program house between 2004 and 2006. My CNSP connection began with the Nepali language training I received in 2002 from Banu Oja and Shambu Oja and led to the academic advice and friendly companionship of Kathryn March, David Holmburg, Dambar Chemjong, and Tunga Sampang Rai. Finally, I thank both Dambar Chemjong and Manisha Adhikhari for their assistance in creating English translations of Nepali language documents produced by members of Nepal's associations of Deaf people.

Since leaving Michigan I have been teaching at Oberlin College, where engagement with my students inspired me to write a book accessible to a nonspecialist audience and gave me the skills to do so. Quinn Donover and Elana Jacobs-Pontecorvo, by inviting me to speak about Nepal to their student-led American Sign Language class, created the context in which I stumbled on the structure for this book. Additionally, they were fantastic research assistants on a trip to Nepal in 2015 and provided helpful comments on drafts of the manuscript. Hudson Bailey and Ray Gergen also took the time to read chapters and offer careful notes. My excellent colleagues at Oberlin have also supported my fieldwork, analysis, writing, and general well-being; I especially thank Crystal Biruk, Julia Christensen, Judi Davidson, Wendy Beth Hyman, and Baron Pineda.

Colleagues at other institutions have offered important support as well. By providing weekly structure and detailed feedback, members of my writing group, including Susan Frekko, Sarah Hillewaert, Michele Koven, Valentina Pagliai, Jennifer Reynolds, and Chantal Tetreault, have helped me move forward with and refine all of my publications, including this book. Alexandra Jaffe and Paul Garrett offered me the position of book review editor at the *Journal of Linguistic Anthropology* and in so doing gave me an opportunity to think at length about the characteristics of successful monographs. Christopher Berk, Judith Irvine, Ujin Kim, Michael Lempert, Sandhya Narayanan, Chip Zuckerman, and other participants in the Michigan Linguistic Anthropology Lab made very useful observations on selections from the book. Christopher Berk went on to provide insightful comments on a full draft of the manuscript. Constantine Nakassis encouraged me to pursue publishing this research in book form. Chaise LaDousa has unfailingly offered support, advice, and inspiration throughout my career. Gretchen and Ethan Davidson provided a quiet retreat for writing. I am grateful to Carol Hoke, Katie Lee, Deirdre Mullervy, and Ivey Wallace at Gallaudet University Press for their efforts to produce this book.

Above all, I thank the members of Nepal's associations of Deaf people for their friendship, hospitality, and patience. I am indebted to Kiran Acharya, Kalpana Bajracharya, Dinesh K. C. Dhital, Amir Gurung, Raghav Bir Joshi, Upendra Khanal, Jaya Bikash Maharjan, Shyam Kharel,

Suresh Shahi, Pooja Shrestha, Sanjeet Shrestha, Shrij Shrestha, Tulasi Das Shrestha, Uday Bahadur Shrestha, Deepak Shakya, Pramila Shakya, Devendra Shakya, Pratigya Shakya, Surjan Shakya, Dipawali Sharmacharya, and Cheeri Sherpa, along with many others.

Finally, I thank my family—Aaron, Leo, and Sylvia Dilloway; Randi Hoffmann, Lee T. Hoffmann Sr., Lee Thomas Hoffmann Jr.; and Ann and Jerry Dilloway—for their love and patience.

I alone am responsible for any errors.

A Note on Transliteration, Pronunciation, and Transcription

ALTHOUGH THE NEPALI LANGUAGE is usually written using the Devanagari script, in this book I have transliterated Nepali terms into Roman script. In so doing I have followed Ahearn (2001) in adopting Turner's ([1931] 1990) transliteration conventions and in replacing Turner's *c* with *ch* and his *ch* with *chh*. Nepali terms are italicized on their first occurrence. Because the pronunciation of Nepali words may not be obvious to all speakers, I share an excerpt from Ahearn's (2001) pronunciation guide:

a	as in *fun*
ā	as in *cot*
i	as in *peek*
u	as in *pool*
e	as in *pay*
ai	as in *guy*
o	as in *moan*
ou	as in *sew*

Moreover, "consonants are pronounced approximately the same as their English counterparts, with the exception of the *t*s and *d*s, which have dental aspirated and unaspirated phonemes (represented by *th, dh, t, d*) and retroflexed aspirated and unaspirated phonemes (represented by *ṭh, ḍh, ṭh, ḍh*) . . . [S]everal other consonants come in aspirated and unaspirated phonemes; these are represented in the book by the presence of an *h* (as in *gh* or *bh*), which indicates that more breath should be added to the consonant" (Ahearn 2001, xvi).

Following Gallaudet University Press guidelines, I place the glosses of sign language terms in small caps.

Signing and Belonging in Nepal

"I See That You Are Deaf"

FIGURES 1 AND 2 portray deaf Nepalis moving through a public place. The first image shows a mother, a father, and a child walking down a street (the traffic light suggests an urban context, possibly Kathmandu, Nepal's capital city). As they walk past couples chatting and shopkeepers interacting with their customers, the parents take pains to silence their deaf son (as his vocalizations would likely make his deafness apparent) and prevent him from using his hands to gesture or sign (which would likewise reveal his deafness). The son looks confused and disturbed. In the second drawing, the same family is walking down the same street, but in this instance the parents and the child are happily using sign language to communicate with each other in public. Readers will notice, however, that, rather than going

Figure 1

Figure 2

about their business as in the first drawing, the bystanders have all stopped what they were doing to gawk at the signing family, looking shocked and displeased.

Pratigya Shakya,[1] a Deaf[2] Nepali artist, produced these drawings, which capture important aspects of Deaf social life in Nepal during the historical period I describe in this book: that of a decade-long civil war (1996–2006)

---

1. Following anthropological convention, most of the given names in this text are pseudonyms. However, I have used real names in the case of well-known public figures, such as Pratigya Shakya. Throughout the book, if I include a last name in identifying a person, I am using the person's actual name. If I use only a first name, it is a pseudonym.

2. As will be discussed in detail later in the chapter, in this book I follow the common Deaf Studies convention of writing the English word "deaf" in lowercase to indicate the inability to hear, "Deaf," written with a capital D, to indicate identification as a member of a signing community, and using the mixed case, d/Deaf, to refer to groups or situations in which both biological and cultural framings of d/Deafness are relevant. As this book will make clear, my use of this convention

that transformed the Hindu Kingdom into a secular republic. At that time, many deaf Nepalis, particularly those in urban centers, had begun to adopt and promote the idea that Deaf signers constituted a distinct, but marginalized, ethnolinguistic group, identified and constituted by the use of a particular language, Nepali Sign Language (NSL). Within this model, one's status as Deaf was thus not based on an inability to hear per se but on competence in a sign language and engagement in Deaf social networks. These networks extended beyond Nepal, as local associations of Deaf people formed social, financial, and ideological relationships with a range of international Deaf persons and organizations that had been instrumental in introducing this framework to the country.

From an ethnolinguistic perspective, a person should not hide their Deafness; rather, through displays of NSL use it was possible to claim membership in a social group both close knit and far ranging. However, even as this understanding of Deafness had been adopted and championed by members of Deaf social networks in primarily urban settings, deafness continued to carry highly negative connotations for the hearing majority: "seeing that someone was d/Deaf" could have a wide range of social consequences in Nepal.

Indeed, although organizations of Deaf people around the globe were increasingly adopting ethnolinguistic framings of Deafness, leading some to speak of an emerging transnational "Deaf-World" (e.g., Lane 2005), the meanings and consequences of this perspective varied within and across cultural contexts (Monaghan et al. 2003; Friedner and Kusters 2014). For example, in the United States, ethnolinguistic understandings of Deafness emerged in contrast to a biomedical perspective, in which deafness was seen as a physical disability.[3] However, a biomedical framework was not the most widespread alternative understanding of the nature and consequences of deafness in Nepal. Though this perspective was salient in some parts of the country, the most common alternative belief was that an inability to hear was the result of bad karma, or misdeeds in a previous life. Karma was

---

should not be taken to imply that I view this distinction as relevant in the same ways across social contexts.

3. See Baynton (1996) for a more complex account of how understandings of deafness have varied and shifted in the United States over time.

thought to influence a person's relative degree of personal purity or pollution, which could be transmitted to others through contact. As a result, deafness was highly stigmatized, and deaf persons were often shunned.

These different binaries (ethnolinguistic vs. biomedical; ethnolinguistic vs. karmic) were reflected and reproduced by the different terms used to refer to d/Deaf persons in these settings. In the United States (and indeed, in this book), a terminological distinction is often made in writing between the terms "deaf" and "Deaf." The uncapitalized spelling refers only to audiological impairment, whereas the capitalized version indicates self-identification as a member of a signing community. The d/Deaf distinction in the United States thus contrasted disability and ethnolinguistic frameworks, in which "deaf" was typically (mis)understood by hearing speakers as a socially neutral term.

In Nepal, on the other hand, different understandings of d/Deafness were often mapped onto distinct Nepali-language terms: *lāṭo* and *bahirā* (or *bahiro*). Lāṭo, a pejorative term meaning "deaf and dumb" in the literal and the figurative senses, reflected the stigma surrounding deafness. Deaf leaders often pointed out that the term lāṭo indicated a lack of communicative or intellectual ability rather than simply hearing loss; signers, therefore, were exempted from such a state and should be referred to as bahirā. Broadly, bahirā connoted a more positive view of d/Deaf people and often an alignment with an ethnolinguistic perspective on Deafness as well.

Lāṭo was by far the most widely known term among hearing Nepalis during my research. For example, in 2005 I traveled through Mustang (a remote mountainous region in the north of Nepal), searching for deaf persons for an informal survey I was conducting for the National Federation of the Deaf Nepal. On reaching each village, I would ask whether any *bahirā mānchhe* (deaf people) were in residence. I usually received a blank stare or a negative response. But if I used the term lāṭo, my interlocutor would often indicate understanding and reply that there were "dumb" people living in the village.[4] This posed a problem: Understandably, the term *lāṭo* had become highly politicized by the associations of Deaf people in Kathmandu as a symbol of the larger society's negative characterization of deafness.

---

4. Taylor (1997) reports the same experience in her travelogue on d/Deafness in Nepal.

Groups such as the Kathmandu Association of the Deaf had campaigned vigorously to remove the term from media accounts that focused on their activities. Accordingly, I felt very uncomfortable using the term *lāṭo* even though its alternative, *bahirā,* was often not understood in the villages I was visiting. Ultimately I settled on an awkward formulation, *kān-na-suune mānchhe* ("people whose ears do not hear"), supplemented occasionally with *mukh-na-bolne mānchhe* ("people whose mouths do not speak").

The predominance of the term *lāṭo* was not restricted to rural areas. During my first trip to Nepal in 1997, and on later visits in 2001 and 2004–2006, when I would walk down the street chatting in NSL with Deaf friends in Kathmandu, the hearing people we passed would often gape (as in Shakya's illustration) and make comments about us, assuming that I was deaf or that, as a *videshi* (foreigner), I would not understand their spoken Nepali. I overhead observers almost exclusively use the stigmatizing term *lāṭo* while discussing us.[5] Such a situation, in which outsiders do not use a group's preferred ethnonym (name used to refer to an ethnic group), out of refusal or ignorance, was an experience shared by many other stigmatized ethnolinguistic groups in Nepal.[6]

Though the karmic and ethnolinguistic framings of d/Deafness might seem diametrically opposed, attention to the convergence of, as well as contrasts between, these models is necessary to understand the social transformations through which Nepal's Deaf community has emerged and continues to grow and change. For example, although d/Deaf Nepalis were often believed to be capable of polluting others, they were not unique in this respect: During the period in which Deaf Nepalis began to adopt and enact an ethnolinguistic model of Deafness, most social groups in Nepal were associated with hierarchically ranked degrees of pollution or purity, believed to derive from karma, which could likewise be transmitted

---

5. On a trip in 2015, I found that younger people in Kathmandu had begun to use the term *bahirā* or *bahiro* when speculating about my friends and me as we walked down the street while signing. However, occasionally their older companions would not understand the term and would need it translated into the term *lāṭo.*

6. For example, while Thangmi is their preferred ethnonym, this group was often referred to as the Thami (Shneiderman and Turin 2006).

through interaction. For example, if a hearing person was born into a low-caste social group that was associated with pollution, this, too, was considered a karmic consequence. Accordingly, to describe Deaf people as an ethnolinguistic group did not in and of itself refute an association with bad karma and pollution. As I show in chapter 3, to combat this stigma, leaders of the associations of Deaf people sought to link a standardized NSL—and with it an emerging Deaf social category—with practices and symbols of high-caste Hinduism that connoted good karma and purity.

These efforts were also responsive to the political situation in Nepal during the historical era (1997–2006) described in this book. This period was a time of increased political mobilization by many of the country's marginalized ethnolinguistic groups, who protested that the state's framing of Nepali nationalism was grounded in symbols and practices that marginalized them. This tension was one important driver of the Maoist "People's War", which ravaged the country from 1996 to 2006 and ultimately led to the aforementioned transition of the country from a Hindu kingdom to a secular republic. One of the primary means by which such ethnic groups defined themselves was through the claim of a mother tongue other than Nepali. As Deaf Nepalis adopted an ethnolinguistic model of deafness, they became potentially aligned with other marginalized, but increasingly politically active, ethnolinguistic groups in Nepal. This alignment risked exposing them to the governmental discrimination and oppression such groups often encountered during that period. Deaf leaders' efforts to associate NSL with high-caste practices also linked the language to Nepali nationalism, thereby making Deaf identity politics less subject to repression by the state. At the same time, however, the standardization project complicated the ability of some Deaf Nepalis to simultaneously affiliate with Deaf and birth social networks.

Similarly, a given person's inclusion in a Deaf category was determined by the intersection of ethnolinguistic and karmic understandings of personhood. The stigma of deafness in Nepal could lead to the social and linguistic isolation of deaf children, such that some were not able to acquire language in childhood. Those who were first exposed to NSL in adulthood were often highly constrained in their ability to learn the language. Accordingly, their inclusion in a Deaf social category could be problematic. However, just as the ritual pollution associated with deafness could be shared through social contact, so could other qualities such as competence. By copying the signs of competent signers, some such Nepalis were permitted to share that competence and partake in a Deaf identity based in NSL (see chapter 4).

Interactions between karmic and ethnolinguistic models of d/Deafness in Nepal also affected hearing Nepalis who interacted with Deaf signers. At the time of my research, the dominant understanding was that deaf people transmitted ritual pollution to hearing people. Despite that widespread belief, and despite the fact that food was an especially effective medium for the transmission of such pollution, from 1997 on a popular restaurant chain in Kathmandu began to hire Deaf waitstaff and prominently advertise their presence. While karma and the attendant belief in ritual pollution were significant idioms for structuring social relations, during the period under discussion, *bikās* (development), class, and modernity had come gradually to coexist and/or compete with karma as important social frameworks. By taking food from servers traditionally considered polluted and, increasingly, using NSL signs to place orders, hearing clientele could demonstrate *bikāsi* ("developed," in contrast to "undeveloped" or "backward") qualities by rejecting the ritual pollution model (see chapter 5). This practice simultaneously combated and reinforced the stigma surrounding deafness during this period.

The primary argument of this book is thus that, rather than outright rejecting local understandings of personhood and social groups based in notions of karma and transmissible purity and pollution, Deaf signers employed them in producing Deafness as an ethnolinguistic category in Nepal. Indeed, as the following chapters show, both the ethnolinguistic and karmic models of d/Deafness ultimately drew on the same basic premise: that persons and larger social formations are mutually constituted through interaction. Further, just as the framing of NSL and Deaf as mutually constitutive drew on both contrasts and convergences between models for understanding d/Deafness, the meanings and effects of such interactive processes hinged on both similarity and variation in embodied practices, including language use.

I Enter (with a Smile)

I first developed relationships with Deaf signers in Nepal in 1997, when I was twenty years old, during an undergraduate semester abroad. A hearing American, I had been studying American Sign Language (ASL) at my home institution for several years. That training had disabused me of many oddly popular and persistent myths, such as the notion of the existence of a single universal sign language. Therefore, after getting settled in Kathmandu, I made inquiries about whether there were any associations of Deaf people in the city that might offer lessons in a local sign language. A friend of one of my Nepali language teachers passed along the address, not far from my homestay in the Naxal neighborhood, of the Kathmandu Association of the Deaf (KAD).

Just past a heavily trafficked intersection, where cars and motorcycles flowed around a tree housing a temple in the middle of the street, I found an alleyway marked by a small blue metal sign bearing the KAD's logo. The alley opened into a residential courtyard, from which a small white dog came bounding, barking and blocking my way. I was a bit afraid of dogs, so I hesitated, thus encouraging it to growl more aggressively. I considered retreating to the main road and trying my luck another time. However, though the sunny day did not allow me to see through the windows and open door into the relatively dim interior of KAD, I could hear sounds of people interacting within.[7] Realizing that it was possible that association members inside might observe me being chased away by the dog, I pulled myself together and continued to the entrance (with the dog only feinting at my leg. That dog remained my nemesis for some time). I entered, grinning awkwardly and laughing to mask my embarrassment both at being afraid of the dog and my shyness about entering the KAD without introduction.

Inside it was cool and dim, compared to the hot sunny autumn afternoon. The room was lined with benches and chairs, to the left of the door a desk, and to the right an entry to a private office. About fifteen people were there that day, seated in the chairs circling the room, chatting together in sign language. After a *namaste*, a gesture of greeting used by most Nepalis, I introduced myself using ASL. (I later learned that my use of ASL had helped settle the debate that had been going on inside about my country of origin; I *had* been observed with the dog in the alley.) A young woman approached me and replied in ASL that I was welcome to take a course in NSL. This woman, Amita, took me aside, and, through a mixture of ASL, English fingerspelling (manual representations of the letters of the alphabet), and written English, we arranged for me to attend NSL classes in the afternoons. I was asked to sign a guestbook, in which I saw notes from d/Deaf and hearing

---

7. Deaf signers are not necessarily silent and can use sound as a strategic resource (e.g., vocalizing or banging on a table to attract attention via sound or vibration).

visitors from a wide range of countries. Then I waved good-bye to all, again braved the scary dog, and reemerged into the bright light of the alley.

A fairly shy person, I had been nervous during this first encounter. I had anxiously wondered: Would I be able to explain what I wanted? Would classes even be available? Would I be welcome to participate or would I be imposing? Would the dog bite me on the way out? Consequently, as mentioned earlier, I spent the duration of that brief encounter smiling widely and occasionally laughing in order to both indicate and smooth over my nervousness. This habit may seem quite natural to readers whose cultural backgrounds are similar to mine. However, I learned that such smiling was by no means a universal communicative strategy. Nepalis did not habitually grin and laugh when nervous, nor did they typically smile in photographs. That is not to say that Nepalis were grim or humorless—far from it—but rather that laughing and grinning were reserved for a smaller range of interactive contexts that were specifically about humor or joy rather

Figure 3   My husband smiling for a photo on his first day visiting Nepal, while I try hard to suppress the urge to smile (and only partially succeed), along with Nepali friends posing with typical serious faces.

than serving as a default facial expression or one that was appropriate when one was nervous. (See figure 3 for an illustration of this cultural contrast.)

After a few months of studying NSL and forming friendships at the KAD, I was given a name sign that related to my (from a Nepali perspective) excessive smiling. Name signs are signed alternatives to spoken language names, typically created and bestowed by Deaf peers.[8] Names signs sometimes had an initialized component (that is, a hand formed into the shape of the fingerspelled letter with which the signer's written name began). The form of name signs also typically related to some distinctive physical feature or notable habitual activity of the person named. For example, an initialized handshape might be located near a salient physical feature (e.g., a scar, birthmark, or unusually large ears) or performed in a manner suggestive of a characteristic activity (e.g., flipping one's hair out of one's eyes).

These physically descriptive signs could take forms that may have seemed insulting to outsiders but were understood in positive terms by insiders. For example, some Deaf Nepalis had sign names that suggested a runny nose (e.g., an initialized handshape performed below the nostrils, with a short movement down toward the lips). Although Deaf adults would certainly not allow snot to run freely down their face, many were proud of such a sign name because it suggested that they had entered into Deaf social life at a very young age as, literally, a "snot-nosed kid." The name sign I was given took the form of an American English fingerspelled letter E to mark my American nationality (as opposed to an initialized form from the NSL fingerspelling system, based on the locally dominant Devanagari script), located at the side of an exaggeratedly grinning mouth. Thus, this name sign drew attention to my habit of smiling at inappropriate times.

---

8. When referring to Deaf friends in this book, the pseudonyms I use are based on spoken Nepali names rather than sign names even though I used the latter to refer to them in practice. This is because I cannot describe sign names while preserving anonymity and because assigning arbitrary sign names would suggest inaccurate social or physical information about the person so named. This is not to say that spoken language names do not also imply social information (such as caste or ethnic membership). However, such implications are less highly specific than is the case for sign names.

When I was given this name in 1997, none of us had heard of email. However, my initial visit to the KAD led to the formation of a set of relationships that have now endured for nearly two decades. During that time the world has changed in many ways, not least via the worldwide spread of Internet access. The NSL sign that was eventually coined to refer to email closely resembled my name sign: an English fingerspelled E positioned at the side of the signer's mouth, often but optionally followed by a movement resembling typing on a keyboard.[9] During my first visits to Nepal after this sign emerged, I constantly saw from the corner of my eye people signing what appeared to be my name, whipped to attention, and then realized that they were not discussing me after all. My confusion was exacerbated by the fact that, over time, the exaggerated smiling element of my name had softened, either reflecting my increasing adaptation to local facial expression norms or (more likely) the fact that my friends had grown accustomed to my habit of smiling inappropriately, such that it became less noticeable to them. Accordingly, my name and the sign for email became increasingly similar. As a result, many Deaf Nepali friends I made in later years, who had not known me in the 1990s, assumed that my name sign had indeed sprung from an association with email (perhaps because, during the time I spent in the United States, I remained in contact with Deaf friends in Nepal via that medium). How a given person interpreted the origin of my name sign indicated the time depth of our relationship.

The ways in which my name sign emerged and changed over time (in both its form and people's interpretations of its significance) illustrate that language is not a static phenomenon independent of human relationships but that linguistic forms and structures, as well as their meanings and effects, emerge from, reflect, and affect social interactions and relationships. Indeed, this book is full of situations in which people try to make sense of linguistic forms by linking them to social information about a person or group of people, as well as situations in which people creatively manipulate linguistic forms to effect social change.

---

9. The form EMAIL represented in the 2003 version of the NSL dictionary did not include the initialized E. Nevertheless, the version described in the text is the one I observed signers using most frequently.

Theoretical and Methodological Approach

This understanding of the nature of language led me to and was refined by my graduate training in linguistic anthropology, which treats language as a culturally situated practice. Although, whenever possible, I avoid using the technical terminology of my field in this book (we linguistic anthropologists are known for our jargon!), I explain key theoretical concepts. Most fundamentally, I expand on what I mean in this book when I write about "language." As a linguistic anthropologist, when I talk about a language such as English or NSL, I mean something different from what a layperson (or even someone from a related discipline such as linguistics) might. I do not treat languages as discrete and homogeneous bundles of linguistic structures imagined to both exist independently of and be uniformly shared by a community of speakers. Instead, I approach language as practice rather than product, something that informs and emerges from people's social interactions. Even though there is certainly a great deal of overlap between what people who we would say use "the same" language do in their interactions, no one uses and understands language in exactly the same way.

Rather, each person has a particular "linguistic repertoire," that is, specific ways of using and interpreting linguistic forms (Gumperz 1965; Blommaert and Backus 2011; Benor 2010; Rymes 2014). Such repertoires never represent the entirety of what people typically call "a language," such as French or Spanish (e.g., we can consider someone fluent in English even if the person is not familiar with all varieties of English or all sets of arcane professional terminologies), nor are they restricted by language boundaries (linguistic repertoires are always—to varying degrees—multilingual and include the ability to use or recognize elements of languages a person might not claim to fully know). These repertoires differ according to people's particular biographical histories. At the same time, lest I be seen as promoting a view of language as a property of individuals, I must stress that the development and deployment of linguistic repertoires are fundamentally social processes.

Variation in how people use language is not a design flaw but is instead central to how linguistic and social meanings emerge in context. That is, although in some cases diversity in how we use language can lead to misunderstandings (e.g., Gumperz 1982; Bailey 1997), more often such variation is a vital communicative resource. For example, differences in how people speak can provide clues about their identity and/or their stance on a given situation (e.g., my use of ASL and habit of smiling suggested my American citizenship to the members of the KAD). The ways in which language use can be taken as pointing to social and cultural contexts is one of the primary intersections between linguistic and social relations. However, variation in language use does not simply map onto preexisting identities, groups, or stances but is also a primary means of producing such social formations (Silverstein 1976, 1979). Linguistic anthropologists call the phenomenon of using language to both point to and create context "social indexicality" (Ochs 1993; Silverstein 1976).

In my introductory course in linguistic anthropology at Oberlin College (Hoffmann-Dilloway 2009), I often illustrate this concept for the class by playing random clips of English speakers talking, and then I ask students to tell me what they can infer about the speakers not only from *what* they say but also from *how* they say it. By interpreting differences in pronunciation, word choices, and grammatical structures, students offer a rich set of guesses about the age, geographical origin, gender, occupation, ethnicity, state of mind, activity, social class, and other aspects of the speakers just from decontextualized audio clips (here I am using a spoken example, but signed languages are just as characterized by variation yielding social indexicality).[10] In more fully contextualized interactions, people have an even richer set of meaningful clues to work with. Their inferences are derived precisely from variation; we could not make such guesses if everyone used language in precisely the same way all the time.

However, it is not only how people produce language that varies but also how people interpret the significance of those forms. These different interpretations themselves provide meaningful clues about a person. The ability of KAD members to recognize my signing as ASL indicated their past exposure to d/Deaf signers from the United States. Likewise, someone's understanding of the origin of my name sign revealed something about our relationship. Or, to return to the example from my classroom, when I play a clip of a speaker, students' guesses do not just reflect differences in how

---

10. With regard to NSL in particular, Khanal (2013a, 2013b) has studied both age-related and regional variation in the language.

the speakers talk but also reveal differences in the students' backgrounds, as their histories affect the ways in which they interpret the clip.

For example, most of my students will identify some speakers as being from what they understand to be the American South. But which clips they identify as such can reveal where they themselves are from, as what constitutes "the South" varies according to social setting. Furthermore, if a student can offer more fine-grained guesses about a speaker's origin, placing the person in a particular region, state, or even city, I am usually correct in guessing that the student is also from that region or has spent significant time there. Alternatively, some students will guess that a speaker with what they perceive as a Southern accent is from a lower social class due to the students' exposure to linguistic stereotypes in the media (exposure to media is also a part of their biographical histories [e.g., Spitulnik 1996; Meek 2006]). Variation in how my students interpret "Southern" accents allows us to discuss how this social category is produced. "Southernness" is not an objective or natural category that students can simply recognize but is instead produced through such socially situated assessments.

An important task for a linguistic anthropologist is thus to explore both the processes by which people come to their particular interpretations of the social indexicalities of linguistic forms and the effects of these interpretations. Such interpretations, whether conscious or operating below conscious awareness, can indeed be very consequential, as people make deep social, political, economic, and emotional investments in their understandings of the significance of different kinds of language use. For example, social gatekeepers' assessments of language can facilitate or limit people's access to resources such as jobs or citizenship.

These indexical interpretations can crystallize into or be derived from broader language ideologies, the "ubiquitous set of diverse beliefs," whether implicit or explicit, which are "used by speakers of all types as models for constructing linguistic evaluations and engaging in communicative activity" (Kroskrity 2004, 497). Language ideologies are both a means by which people rationalize the indexical connections they perceive between language use and users and a filter through which they discern particular indexical connections. This typically involves a process called *iconization*, an ideological framing of a given language or linguistic feature as formally congruent with an associated social group, thereby naturalizing or essentializing such links (Irvine and Gal 2000).

Language ideologies include both scholarly theories and people's casual opinions of or feelings about language. They might focus on language broadly (e.g., claims that humans are the only species to use language), particular languages (e.g., opinions that some languages sound "beautiful" while others sound "ugly"), or specific aspects of language structure or use (e.g., a belief that double negatives are illogical and should not be used) (Ahearn 2012, 21). Language ideologies are loaded with "moral and political interests" (Irvine 1989, 225). That is, because beliefs about language always carry implications about speakers, they typically serve the interests of some social groups over others.

One common and deeply consequential language ideology is the "linguistic monolith" understanding of languages that I briefly invoked and rejected earlier. This is the notion that languages are (or should be) discrete, internally homogenous, and map onto likewise discrete and homogeneous communities of speakers (Irvine and Gal 2000; Makoni and Pennycook 2007; Rymes 2014). Although I argue that this perspective is not accurate, this language ideology requires study because it has been a powerful resource in the creation and maintenance of identity politics at various levels, including but not limited to the national (e.g., as governments may insist on the dominance of a single national language to promote national unity) and the ethnic (e.g., as minority groups may use a minority language as an emblem in resisting oppression by national governments). Both Nepal's government and its marginalized ethnic groups have harnessed a linguistic monolith understanding of language in precisely these ways.

A linguistic monolith ideology has also been both harnessed and critiqued by those promoting a view of Deaf people as an ethnolinguistic group. Sign languages often were, and in some settings still are, mistaken to be simple gestures, outside the provenance of human language (Baynton 1996). This ideological perspective has had devastating consequences for many d/Deaf persons. In the 1960s, however, William Stokoe drew on structural linguistic theory to demonstrate that, because signed languages could be described according to the same criteria linguists used for spoken language analysis, they were in fact fully linguistic systems (Stokoe 1960). Such research has been a major factor in the social validation of both sign languages and their users. However, in social settings in which a linguistic monolith understanding of language dominates, many scholars and activists have stressed a given sign language's purportedly discrete and homogeneous nature to defend its status as a bona fide language. Variation within and contact between sign languages, as well as contact between signed and spoken languages (via signers' complex linguistic repertoires), can be rendered invisible by this perspective. For example, scholars have only recently begun incorporating into their descriptions of ASL varieties that emerged in racially segregated schools for deaf students in the United States and asking whether and how these varieties relate to different varieties of English (McCaskill et al. 2011).

A linguistic monolith perspective is not the only ideological framework through which sign languages and their role in constituting d/Deaf sociality has been understood (e.g., Brueggemann 2009). For example, Wrigley (1996, 104) has argued that what he calls "deaf citizenship" inheres in "a process, in social relations. This citizenship is not a static commodity of deafness or of sign language as a modality: it lies in the social exchange of recognition produced through signing." Similarly, in this book I approach NSL as a collection of overlapping but diverse practices, whereby recognition, belonging, and distinction within a Nepali Deaf social category are indexically produced. Ultimately, this book shows how both personas and larger social formations such as ethnolinguistic identity (e.g., Deaf) or nationality (e.g., Nepali) affect and emerge from interactive language use, while closely attending to rather than erasing all of the rich variation that entails. I further ask how these processes are mediated by participants' ideological understandings of the relationship between the linguistic and the social, which treat that variation sometimes as a problem and sometimes as a resource (Rosa 2014).

Methodologically, this entailed my not only paying attention to what people explicitly said about the relationship between language and social groups but also closely analyzing how people signed in multiple contexts and how they interpreted that signing (an important source of evidence for such interpretations is how interactions unfold since we cannot read minds) (Sidnell and Enfield 2012). Such analysis requires a good deal of cultural and linguistic competence, which I worked to develop by participating in Deaf social life in Nepal. I acquired my linguistic skills in NSL in part through explicit classroom instruction, which began after my first visit to the KAD. Because the vast majority of deaf Nepalis were born to hearing parents who rarely learned to sign, a common question Deaf Nepalis asked one another on first meeting was "who taught you to sign?" I was lucky to have three excellent early NSL instructors, Amita, Shrihari, and Birendra (all of whom appear at various times throughout this book).

However, my competence in NSL and Deaf cultural life emerged primarily from years of intensive social interaction via signing: chatting at associations of Deaf persons, schools for d/Deaf students, businesses that Deaf persons owned or worked for, and the homes of Deaf friends. Additionally, in 2004 and 2005 I videotaped approximately forty hours of footage of signed conversations and interviews, which I closely analyzed, often with help from signers in Nepal. Though readers should look to my journal articles for more detailed linguistic analyses (Hoffmann-Dilloway 2008, 2010, 2011a, 2011b), the arguments in this book have emerged from these materials.

Just as my language skills emerged primarily from social interactions, the same is true of the data and analyses I present here. My relationships with Deaf signers in Nepal have been mediated by my role as a researcher but in many cases have also been some of the longest-lasting friendships in my life. Thus, in this book I frequently refer to particular Deaf Nepalis as my friends. Some readers may wonder whether that is an appropriate term to use in an academic study. Might friendships with research participants skew my findings? However, rather than write in a style that erases my social positionality in Nepal in order to represent my findings as "pure," "objective," or "raw," I want to make clear to the reader that my research (like all ethnographic research) is produced not in spite of, but through, relationships, with all the complexities and obligations they entail. As medical anthropologist Crystal Biruk, my colleague and, in fact, friend puts it in a book in progress, my data are "cooked" (by the social and cultural processes through which they were gathered) rather than "raw" (purified of such social and cultural entailments). However, truly "raw" data do not exist; by signaling the social mediation of my arguments, I hope to provide the reader additional critical insight into the processes by which they emerged.

Due to constraints on travel imposed by the war (1996–2006), which co-occurred almost exactly with the period in which my primary research trips took place (1997–2006), the majority of these interactions were conducted and recorded in the Kathmandu Valley, home to the country's capital city and a major center for Deaf social life. However, more than twenty regional associations of Deaf people were active in the country, organized under an umbrella institution known at the time of my research as the National Federation of the Deaf and Hard of Hearing (NFDH) and renamed in 2011 as the National Federation of the Deaf Nepal (NDFN).[11] I was able to interact with Deaf Nepalis in a wide range of sites in this geographically diverse country, from the high mountains in the arid northern Mustang region bordering Tibet, to the middle-hills lake town of Pokhara, to the flat, hot, southern Terai region on the border with India.

In addition to being geographically diverse, Nepal has been characterized by a great deal of social, cultural, and linguistic diversity. Broadly speaking, four major politically salient sociocultural groups were active in the country, none of which formed a majority and each of which contained a great deal of internal variation. The politically dominant group consisted of high-caste Hindus from the middle-hills region of the country (at 30.89 percent of the population). Two other major groups were the Dalits (low-caste Hindus, 14.99 percent) and the Madhesis (castes and tribal groups from the Terai region, 32.29 percent). The fourth major grouping consisted of the *ādivāsi janajāti* (indigenous nationalities, 36.31 percent), which included many ethnic groups, such as the Sherpas, Newars, Gurungs, and Magars (Hangen 2007, 4; Lawoti 2005, 99). As the next chapter shows, understanding the historical and political processes by which this social variation was produced and organized is vital for comprehending both attitudes toward deafness and the emergence of Deaf sociality in Nepal.

---

11. The name change highlighted the federation's focus on culturally Deaf activities rather than the mitigation of difficulties for those hard of hearing Nepalis who orient toward spoken language and hearing social networks. The organization goes by the initials NDFN, although these do not reflect the order of the words in its title. This is in order to distinguish the organization from the National Federation of the Disabled Nepal, which uses the initials NFDN (Green 2014).

Historical and Cultural Context 2

ON A 2015 visit to Kathmandu,[12] I reunited with my friend Pramod after a long absence. I was delighted to see him but sad to note that he was dressed all in white, from his shoes to his knit cap: This was an indication that a death had occurred in his immediate family. Pramod explained that his father had passed away months ago and that it was his responsibility to observe a set of mourning practices for the following year. Two of my students from Oberlin College had joined me in Nepal on this trip. They had previously studied ASL in the United States and were using that background to facilitate their study of NSL, which they used to chat with Pramod. Knowing that it was the students' first time in Nepal, he drew on a mixture of ASL (he had experience with the language through contact with d/Deaf signers from abroad; in fact, he had been working as a guide for d/Deaf tourists) and NSL to describe to them the details of the mourning rituals he was observing. Among other things, these practices entailed avoiding certain types of food and keeping his head shaved, aside from a small tuft of hair, called a *sikhā*, on the back of his head. Throughout this discussion, Pramod repeatedly attributed these practices to "Nepali culture." In fact, the sign he used to refer to "culture," which took the form of an index finger wagging behind the signer's head, was often understood to be motivated by resemblance to the *sikhā*.

During the subsequent days we spent together, Pramod and other Deaf friends frequently anticipated moments when my students might be confused by the goings-on and hurried to provide them with explanations, usually with explicit reference to Nepali culture. Often these moments centered on food and drink. For instance, the American students and I tended to carry personal refillable water bottles with us, which we drank

---

12. The visit took place in January, before the 2015 earthquake struck Nepal in April.

from by placing our mouths directly on the rim. Our Nepali friends were more apt to share a single bottle and drink by pouring the water into their open mouths from several inches above, never allowing their lips to touch the container. My students were impressed by this skill and likewise attempted to drink this way, drenching their faces (I had given up trying to master this technique long ago).

In explaining this practice to my students, Deaf friends provided different levels of detail. My favorite interpretation, offered by a young man named Kashi, was that young Nepalis were motivated to learn the skill due to the fact that drinking directly from the bottle made them (and, by implication, us) look infantile, like nursing babies. The broader reason for this practice, however, was that once a bottle had touched someone's mouth, it became *jutho,* or ritually impure. Once jutho, the bottle of water could no longer be shared. (Even though this may sound in some ways like Euro-American germ theory, the underlying principles were related primarily to ritual rather than microbial concerns [Eck 1982].)

Ritual impurity was also a factor underlying the mourning rituals Pramod was observing: For a year after his father's death he would remain in a state of impurity, with a variety of implications for his interactions with others during this period. For example, at Nepali meals everyone was typically expected to eat from a separate plate, as once a bite of food had been taken from it, everything remaining was jutho and could not be shared. Different types of food, however, were more or less likely to transmit pollution: One afternoon, Pramod and I attended a party where the host's wife provided a single large platter of french fries, from which guests were free to snack. Because of Pramod's temporarily impure state as a mourner, however, he alone could not take fries from the group platter but was given a small individual plate.

As these examples suggest, ritual pollution could be transmitted between people, sometimes through the mediation of objects such as food items or water bottles. Such pollution could be fleeting and correctable or enduring. In fact, some groups of people, including different castes and ethnic groups—and often d/Deaf persons—were understood to be permanently jutho in relation to other, purer groups. To understand how this concept mediated relationships in Nepal broadly, and specifically influenced d/Deaf lives, it is useful to outline in detail the understandings of the nature of personhood and groups that informed and were affected by practices surrounding ritual pollution, as well as the intersections between these understandings and the broader historical and sociopolitical context in the country.

Porous Personhood

What it means to be a person can vary within and across historical and cultural contexts along a range of dimensions (Shweder and Bourne 1984). For example, what divisions separate one person from another? While Euro-Americans are typically socialized to think of persons as discrete units, bounded by their physical bodies, many in South Asia are raised to perceive persons as porous and relatively unbounded (Dumont 1980; Marriott 1976; Marriott and Inden 1977; Daniel 1984). In fact, Marriot and Inden (1977) contrast the Euro-American notion of the "individual" person with what they call a South Asian "dividual" person: "[D]ividual" persons absorb the substances and qualities of those persons and things around them and likewise affect other persons and things with their own transmittable substance (Marriott 1976). These particulate substances have different characters, including varying degrees of pollution or purity.

Marriott and Inden (1977) based their claims about South Asian personhood on their readings of classic Hindu texts rather than on evidence drawn from daily life in South Asia. Anthropologists who have explored personhood ethnographically have made it clear that the original opposition posed between Euro-American "individuals" and South Asian "dividuals" is overly stark; these broad cultural differences in conceptions of personhood do not prevent those in South Asia from experiencing themselves as individuals in a range of ways (e.g., Mines 1994; Mines and Gourishankar 1990; Wilce 1998). Likewise, Euro-American personhoods are more socially constituted than discourses promoting individuality might suggest (e.g., Goodwin 2004). However, ethnographic work in South Asia, including my own, also confirms that an understanding of persons as porous and constituted through the exchange of substance is indeed highly relevant in daily life for many people in South Asia, pervasively affecting daily activities and social relations (e.g., Cameron 1998; Hepburn 2002; Parish 1994; Hoffmann-Dilloway 2011a).

During my time in Nepal I observed that those around me devoted much energy to avoiding mixing with things, places, or people whose substance might negatively influence their own substance and pursuing interactions that might positively affect their personhood. A common example of the latter included the act of *pujā,* or worship. This practice took many forms but commonly involved offering to a particular god or goddess a plate of substances, such as food, drink, money, or flowers, that the deity particularly favored (e.g., some gods eat meat, whereas others are vegetarian). For example, figure 4 shows a pujā plate prepared by my friends in offering to the Rato Machhendranath deity. The priest who facilitated this offering would, upon its completion, return to the worshipper a bit of this substance, perhaps a single flower or morsel of food, now considered *prasād* (a gift). Figure 5 shows the prasād returned to me when I participated in the pujā offering to Rato Machhendranath. Consuming a gift that a god or goddess had ritually consumed conferred some of the pure substance of the god or goddess to the worshipper. (Prasād in the form of a flower did not need to be consumed; the benefits were conferred simply through having received the token.)

Figure 4   A *pujā* plate prepared for Rato Machhendranath.

Figure 5   The piece of *prasād* was returned to me following pujā.

As the example I've given indicates, I was occasionally invited to participate in doing pujā myself and partake in this beneficial transmission of substance. I also learned how to manage the impact of my own substance on others. Relevant practices included those with which I opened the chapter: avoiding "contaminating" food or drinks in order to minimize the extent to which my personhood would mingle with those who might also wish to consume the meal or beverage. As an illustration, I realized that my inability to drink like a Nepali without spilling water on my face and down my shirt meant that I had to carry my own private bottle with me. If I did not have my own bottle, and a friend offered me a drink, I would not be able to accept without polluting my friend's bottle by drinking from it and thereby essentially claiming it for myself. Carrying my own water did not entirely solve the problem of my inability to drink like a Nepali, however. This was made painfully clear to me on a hot, dusty uphill hike with a friend, when I pulled out my water to take a needed drink. My companion, a young Nepali woman named Priya, looked longingly at the bottle and asked, "Juṭho cha?" (Is it polluted?) It was: I had drunk water directly from the bottle earlier that morning. The water could not be shared. I then learned that, in order to be sociable and helpful, I ought to carry both a juṭho bottle, from which I could drink directly, and another bottle, from which I should not drink and which could remain unpolluted and shareable.

I also learned never to serve myself from large dishes of common food at meals but rather to wait to be served, as even ladling food from the serving dish to my plate would introduce my personal substance into the common bowl. The person who cooked a meal, however, could not avoid affecting the substance of food or drink: The food absorbs particles from the cook, and so, in turn, does the person to whom the food is served. Thus, it was deemed appropriate to accept the sorts of foods that were particularly good conduits for transmitting substance (often those prepared using water, such as cooked rice) only from persons pure enough that their substance would not negatively affect the person receiving the food.

But how could one determine whether it was appropriate to absorb a particular person's substance? People had to take account of directionality and relationality; that is, someone whose personal substance was less pure could accept cooked rice from someone who was relatively more pure, but not the reverse. The eating of beef was proscribed in Nepal, and, as a foreigner from a *gāi khāne* (cow-eating) country, by most reckonings my substance would be considered less pure than most Nepalis with whom I interacted. However, as I was more frequently in a position to receive food cooked by hosts than to cook for others myself, this was rarely an explicit issue so long as I was considerate in my comportment. (It was also possible that some families participated in a purification rite after eating with me.)

A given person's degree of purity or impurity could change as events rendered the person more or less pure. These events could be cyclical and repeating. A person's purity could fluctuate daily, for instance, due to having engaged in polluting activities such as defecating or purifying activities such as bathing or doing pujā. Longer cycles could also influence a person's purity relative to the people the person regularly interacted with. For example, when I lived with the Shrestha family in Kathmandu, our evening meal was typically cooked and served by the *buhāri* (daughter-in-law). When she was menstruating, however, she was considered too ritually impure to cook or serve the members of the family: Her *sāsu* (mother-in-law) had to take over the task. Less frequent events, such as childbirth, could also temporarily affect a person's substance. For example, if an unpolluted person were to touch a woman who had recently given birth, the former would have to seek purification from ritually pure items, such as *pachagavya,* the "five products of the cow" (Höfer 1979, 62). These products included milk, curds, ghee (clarified butter), urine and dung, all of which were understood to be particularly pure substances. Pachagavya, a combination of all five, was even more purifying.

Though I have been stressing the mediating role of food, water, or touch, spiritual and social interactions were not necessarily seen as different from these more obviously physical engagements and likewise facilitated the mixing of substance (Marriott 1959, 1976). As an illustration, a woman who had recently given birth was ritually polluted, but the baby's father, the father's brother, their classificatory brothers and wives, and their sons and unmarried daughters were often considered polluted as well (Höfer 1979, 62). This was the case even if they had not come into direct contact with the mother or the baby: The social bonds were themselves conduits for polluting substance. This chapter's opening example, concerning Pramod's year-long period of pollution following his father's death, likewise illustrates temporary but relatively long-term pollution mediated by social and spiritual rather than physical relations. However, the ritual pollution associated with persons—and groups—could also be considered permanent. Interactions between members of groups were therefore often informed by the rules for managing the transmission of pollution and purity between persons.

Hierarchically Ranked *Jāts*

Nepalis often understood people to be organized into different *jāts*. This term is frequently translated in English as "caste" and understood to refer to hierarchically ranked, endogamous (intramarrying) groups, often associated with inherited occupations. However, jāt is a much broader concept. A more accurate translation might be "kind" (Marriott and Inden 1977). A given person might simultaneously belong to several overlapping jāts: The term might be used to describe a caste, but it would be equally appropriate to use it to describe members of a gender, race, occupation, or religion, as well as citizens of a particular nation. As a case in point, Nepalis sometimes considered visitors to the country to be members of a "tourist" jāt (Hepburn 2002).

The implication of the concept is that the personal substance of the living things to which the term is applied consists of a common essence (Gellner 1995, 3), which was, as explained earlier, typically understood to be particulate and transmittable to others. Some jāts were seen to inherently and enduringly possess more or less purity than others (Cameron 1998). In Nepal, as in many other South Asian contexts, some jāts were understood to be hierarchically "rankable," according to their degree of purity or pollution, into a system of four *varṇas*, or tiers. These varṇas included Brāhmans or Bāhuns (priestly castes); Chetris (rulers and warriors); Vaisyas (merchants); and Śūdras (servants). Brāhmans/Bāhuns were considered purest caste groups, Śūdras the least. Ranked below Śūdras and even less pure were Dalits, considered "untouchable" or "outcast" due to their hereditary association with highly polluting occupations (e.g., tailors or street sweepers).

Low and outcaste groups were "viewed as realizing the fruits of the sins of previous lifetimes" (Parish 2002, 179). While everyone, high caste or low, continually worked to manage and mitigate the polluting effects of the kinds of temporary pollution described earlier, permanent differences in the degree of pollution between groups also had to be managed in ways that reflected and/or created hierarchies of jāts. For example, though the Shretha family buhāri was not considered pure enough to cook and serve food to her family when menstruating, members of this family would never have wished to accept cooked rice from someone born into a lower-caste jāt.

How did this perspective, largely attributed to Hindu thought and practice, become so prominent in Nepal, a highly ethnically and religiously diverse country? And why did it take on this particular form when Hinduism itself is extremely diverse? Historical and political contexts can affect the constitution of and relations between jāts. For example, much anthropological and historical research has explored how British occupiers strategically shaped understandings of the caste system in India to further their control over the colony (e.g., Dirks 1989; Raheja 1988). Similarly, in Nepal it is possible to trace the political and historical processes by which a particular configuration of relations between jāts arose and was enforced.

While Nepalis have always been exceedingly diverse in ethnic, religious, and linguistic terms, the rulers of the nation have always been Hindu. Prithvi Narayan Shah, the Hindu leader of the Kingdom of Gorkha, unified Nepal in 1769. In an effort to unite as one polity the people occupying the territories he had claimed, he imposed upon the subjects (whether they considered themselves Hindu or not) an encompassing but hierarchically organized caste system, framing the new state as a "garden" with thirty-six flowers (jāts), ranked within the four varṇas. In 1846, Jang Bahadur Rana overthrew the Shah rulers in the Kot massacre and declared himself and his descendants hereditary prime ministers, maintaining the Shah line as powerless figureheads. In 1854, in order to further incorporate his varied subjects into the Hindu cosmology favored by the ruling class, Jang Bahadur Rana created a document called the *Muluki Ain* (General, or National, Code).

Enumerating and ranking Nepal's social groups, the *Muluki Ain* organized Nepal's jāts into broad categories according to their purity as determined by Hindu standards: *tāgādhāri* (sacred thread wearers, meaning upper-caste Hindus), *matwāli* (alcohol drinkers; this category was subdivided into those who could and could not be enslaved); lower-caste groups considered impure but touchable; and those considered untouchable (e.g., Dalits). By specifying in great detail rules for how members of different jāts within these categories could interact and outlining legal consequences for breaking these rules, this legislation further codified and standardized the various, previously relatively fluid, practices concerning jāt relationships in Nepal (Fürer-Haimendorf 1957).

Nationalism and Ethnic Jāts

Nepali leaders' efforts to organize the country's diverse citizens into a single overarching caste hierarchy may be understood in part as a response to Nepal's precarious geopolitical position (between Tibet/China to the north and, at the time of the *Muluki Ain,* British India to the south). By projecting the notion that a Nepali state mapped onto a culturally unified and discrete national population, Jang Bahadur Rana was able to represent Nepal's right to sovereignty in the terms of European Romantic nationalism (Burghart 1984; Höfer 1979). In 1951, the Ranas were unseated by a popular revolution. King Tribhuvan, the then current descendent of the Shah kings, who had been retained as figureheads, was restored to the throne. The kings were expected to participate in a democratic system of government. However, Tribhuvan's successor, King Mahendra, dismissed the elected government in 1960 and established a Panchayat system of autocratic, palace-based, single-party rule.

Though the Panchayat government revised the *Muluki Ain* in 1963 to remove the use of caste as an officially sanctioned method of structuring social relations, the state continued to draw on a Hindu cultural framework in defining its notions of nationalism. National symbols, such as the color red or the image of a cow, were drawn from images associated with caste Hinduism. A common Panchayat-era slogan was "ek bhāṣā, ek besh, ek desh" (one language, one type of clothing, one country) (Hangen 2007). The official language, Nepali, and type of dress referred to by this slogan were those associated with the caste Hill Hindu elite (that is, upper-caste Hindus from the middle hills region of the country, rather than the southern plains) (Lawoti 2005). The emerging educational system was a focal point of efforts to promote a national homogeneity, as all instructional materials were written in Nepali and promoted upper-caste Hindu cultural perspectives (Skinner and Holland 1996). Indeed, an analysis of the standard school texts used in all government schools in the 1980s found that Nepalis were portrayed as uniformly Hindu. When other religions were mentioned, their practitioners were depicted as citizens of other countries (Ahearn 2001, 161).

During the twenty-eight years of one-party Panchayat rule the Nepali government actively worked to repress expressions of non-Hindu identity and activism, which it believed threatened its construal of the nation. Likewise, drawing attention to inequalities among jāts was characterized as politically contentious. In 1990, however, a mass uprising in Kathmandu, called the Jāna Āndolan (People's Movement), ended the Panchayat era, forcing the government to allow the formation of a multiparty parliament and to institute constitutional reforms. During the process of drafting a new constitution, many organizations representing marginalized jāts lobbied the committee to incorporate formal recognition of their rights and to explicitly abolish the grounding of the country's national identity in Hinduism. The Nepali constitution, which had formerly described the nation as "an independent, indivisible, and sovereign monarchical Hindu kingdom," now called it a "multiethnic, multilingual, democratic, independent, indivisible, sovereign, monarchical Hindu kingdom" (His Majesty's Government 1990, article 4[1]). While continuing to characterize Nepal as specifically Hindu, this rewording reflected the government's increased recognition of the political rights of ethnic minorities, a shift that included designating languages other than Nepali as national languages of Nepal and permitting the previously forbidden establishment of ethnic associations.

Many groups in Nepal who had been ranked in the *Muluki Ain* as matwāli and were then erased or marginalized by Nepali nationalism increasingly began to call themselves *ādivāsi janajāti,* or indigenous nationalities. These were largely communities whose identities were linked to languages, religions, and other cultural practices distinct from upper-caste Hinduism and often, but not exclusively, associated with Buddhism and Tibeto-Burman languages. The "English translation of janajāti as 'nationalities' is significant as it emphasizes these communities as 'nations,'" thus challenging a "monolithic construction of Nepal as a Hindu nation"; moreover, the translation of *ādivāsi* as "indigenous" also emphasized "international discourses of indigeneity and indigenous peoples' rights" (Rai 2013, 6). Ādivāsi janajāti were often described as specifically ethnic groups as opposed to caste groups, a terminological shift also likely influenced by Euro-American political discourses (Sharma 1997).

Like castes, ethnic groups are often popularly defined as sociocultural formations that are internally homogeneous, discretely bounded, and endogamous. Ethnicity is sometimes treated as essential or primordial, derived from particular types of bodies (e.g., through the racializing of ethnic practices as stemming from "the blood" or "genetics" [Pagliai 2011] or, in the case of jātis, essential and transmittable substance) and/or derived "naturally" from living in a particular place. Ethnicity may also be popularly understood as grounded in shared cultural practices. Because, as mentioned in chapter 1, languages have frequently been ideologically described as linguistic monoliths, homogeneous and discrete, they have often been referred to as "objective" cultural criteria onto which ethnic boundaries could be mapped. In addition, qualities attributed to language are frequently iconized or understood to be essentially shared by the social group with which they are associated (and vice versa) (Irvine and Gal 2000). Thus, it is often assumed that language and ethnic boundaries naturally coincide.

However, there are no criteria concerning descent or cultural practices—including language—that neatly circumscribe discrete ethnic boundaries (Alonso 1994; Barth 1969; Fishman 1977). Many anthropologists therefore see ethnicity as more a matter of subjective—and affective (Shneiderman 2014)—affiliation than as a set of natural social entities waiting to be discovered. At the same time, it has been important to attend to the ways in which the fluidity implied by this perspective is limited by the conditions that apply in any particular historical and social context. Anthropology's shift from a focus on structure to process (Ortner 1984) has been helpful in this regard, directing scholarly attention less to what ethnicity is (and who "has" it) and more to the ways in which the social utility of the concept is closely associated with processes previously assigned to other domains, such as state development, economic relationships, or ritual practices (Rai 2013; Shneiderman 2014). This focus highlights the power struggles involved in the relational processes of ethnic affiliation and ascription.

Because, in Nepal during the 1990s, ethnic framing of particular jāts emerged in contrast to caste Hinduism, ethnic leaders frequently encouraged their politically active members to reject Hinduism and to highlight Tibeto-Burman elements of their ethnic identities and practices (Fisher 2001). During this period many ādivāsi janajāti ethnic leaders called for their followers to boycott Dasaĩ, a major yearly Hindu festival featuring many rituals that reiterated Nepal's Hindu national identity (Hangen 2005). A number of groups, such as the Dhimal in the Terai, have reshaped events such as weddings to function as sites of indigenous activism (Rai 2013). Many ethnic associations organized language classes to promote the use of languages other than Nepali (Guneratne 2002). Food and drink were also salient symbols used by many to affiliate with or against caste Hindu nationalism. For example, I happened to be vegetarian during the time of my research. When at parties hosted in the home of Deaf or hearing friends born into ādivāsi janajāti families, I was often teasingly called a Bāhun (Hill Brāhman) when I refused snacks such as roasted buffalo. I was able to refute my mock Bāhun status, however, by my willingness to partake in drinking alcohol (as mentioned earlier, the *Muluki Ain* categorized alcohol drinkers below caste Hindus).

Although ethnic organization and activism of the sort described earlier were officially permitted after 1990, tension over the conflict between a Hinduism-based vision of the nation and ethnic diversity within the state remained high, and the marginalization of those who were not caste Hill Hindus (including ādivāsi janajāti, Dalits, and Madhesis) continued. Beginning in 1996, the Maoist People's Liberation Army succeeded in mobilizing many members of these historically oppressed social groups in their effort to achieve "political transformation through an armed revolution" (Rai 2013, 333). The Maoists made central to their platform a goal to end the dominance of high-caste Hinduism in Nepal and to establish a secular state in which previously marginalized groups would have the right to cultural, linguistic, and political self-determination.

Over the course of the ten-year "People's War," Maoist rebels gained control of much of the countryside. Additionally, Maoists were able to put increasing pressure on Kathmandu, the monarchy's stronghold, by calling for and enforcing *banda*s (strikes) in or around the city (as well as elsewhere in the nation). Bandas varied both in length and in the type of activities they forbade. Often they lasted only a day or two and banned only travel by vehicle. But in some cases they lasted as long as a week and banned all movement outside the home. In addition to causing great disruption to the economy, the bandas and blockades demonstrated the Maoists' strength by choking off food and gasoline supplies to the capital. Living in the Kathmandu Valley during this period, I developed the habit of listening—as soon as I woke up each morning (often before opening my eyes)—for the presence or absence of the sound of honking horns, as this would indicate whether a banda was in effect.

Most violent conflicts occurred outside the capital, with villagers taking the brunt of the clashes between the Maoists and the army. Occasionally, however, violence also affected Kathmandu. For example, one afternoon in 2004, I was chatting with friends at the Kathmandu Association of the Deaf when the room shook with the impact of a bomb blast a few streets away. No one was hurt on that occasion, as the building had been evacuated before the explosion. My Deaf friends also recounted frightening encounters with both Maoist rebels and members of the Royal Nepalese Army (who were in the street in great numbers during those years). Fighters from both camps were known to accost people in the streets, demanding contributions or enforcing checkpoints. Because both groups were armed, Deaf signers feared that difficulties in making themselves understood could lead to violence.

They also feared being "overheard" when discussing politically sensitive topics in public. For example, in 2004 old friends cautioned me about changes in the political scene since my last visit (e.g., "it is no longer safe to take shortcuts through the fields in the evening") and taught me two signs for "Maoist," one for use within the associations of Deaf persons and one for use on the streets. The first took the form of hands covering the forehead and mouth (resembling the bandanas that Maoist fighters often wore on their faces to hide their identity). Even many of those unfamiliar with NSL could readily link this sign with images of masked Maoists, which abounded in public newspapers and on the Internet (or/and with people's direct encounters with Maoists). The second sign consisted of an index finger placed first over the chin and then over the forehead, which nonsigners were less likely to interpret as referring to Maoists. Use of this sign was thus less likely to draw negative attention from Maoists or members of the Royal Nepalese Army.

In 2005, in response to his increasingly precarious control of the country, then King Gyandendra dismissed the elected parliament and took unilateral control of the government. Immediately after making this announcement, the king cut off all telephone and Internet connections in the country, ostensibly to hinder Maoists' attempts to organize a response. Although telecommunications resumed after about a week, both freedom of the press and civil liberties were largely dissolved, and human rights abuses were rampant. The king also began imposing frequent curfews in Kathmandu that, like the bandas, severely curtailed the daily lives of residents.

In the spring of 2006, these competing pressures on the daily lives of Kathmandu residents led to an uprising that included an unprecedented number of protesters with a wide range of political and social affiliations. These included the Seven Party Alliance, members of a coalition of Nepali political parties who had been ousted from democratically elected positions by the king's direct rule. To quell the protests, the king declared a "shoot on sight" curfew. In what became known as the Jāna Āndolan II (second People's Movement), the protesters defied the curfew and marched en masse toward the palace despite the presence of the army. This uprising led to an end of the decade-long war, as the Maoists and the Seven Party Alliance signed a peace accord later in 2006. In 2008 the monarchy was abolished altogether, and the country became a secular republic rather than a Hindu kingdom. The Maoist Party (Unified Communist Party of Nepal, Maoist) was incorporated into the reestablished democratic political system. Though I discuss post-2006 developments in the conclusion of this book, the historical period in which Deaf Nepalis adopted international perspectives framing Deaf signers as an ethnolinguistic minority group largely coincided with the period leading up to the war and that of the war, an era in which questions about the role of ethnolinguistic variation in Nepal were especially fraught. How did a Deaf ethnic jāt emerge in and navigate this context?

A Deaf Jāt

A 1990–1991 survey of deafness and ear disease in the country, conducted by the Britain Nepal Otology Service and the Tribhuvan University Teaching Hospital, found that, out of a sample population over the age of five, 16.6 percent of Nepalis had significant loss of hearing while 1.7 percent were profoundly deaf (Little et al. 1993). The most common cause of hearing loss was otitis media, an infection of the middle ear (ibid.; Maharjan et al. 2006). Ragav Bir Joshi (1991), a Deaf Nepali leader, argued that the number of profoundly deaf persons was actually higher, at 3 percent. Nirmal Kumar Devkota (2003), another Deaf Nepali leader, maintained that this percentage may have increased between 1996 and 2006 due to the civil war's disruption of already marginal access to health services.

Moreover, of the cases of hearing loss found in the 1990–1991 survey, 60 percent were initially false negatives (Little et al. 1993). That is, people (or family members speaking for them) reported that they could hear, though testing later showed that they were in fact deaf (ibid.). The stigma associated with deafness, due to the common belief that the condition was the result of the affected person's bad karma, was a significant factor in this underreporting. Like members of other social categories (such as those based on caste or gender), deaf people were often viewed as constituting a jāt; in this case one associated with ritual pollution. How did inclusion in this relatively low-ranking jāt affect simultaneous membership in other jāt categories, such as birth caste? Deaf persons born into higher-ranked castes were sometimes expelled from their birth networks and/or made to engage in polluting tasks, such plowing, which were associated with the impurity usually transmitted along lower-caste lines (Taylor 1997). Deaf Nepalis born into lower-ranking castes or other jāts often faced fewer tensions between deafness and caste membership and could more easily retain their status in each jāt category. For these reasons, many Nepalis interpreted deafness as a low or an outcaste phenomenon, which further reinforced its association with pollution (ibid.).

Given the "dividual" nature of persons, the pollution associated with deafness could be shared with others through regular physical and social contact. As a result, during the period of my research many Nepalis avoided physical and social engagements with d/Deaf persons in order to protect their relatively pure personhoods.[13] For instance, when I interviewed the hearing principal of Kathmandu's Naxal School for the Deaf, she recalled that, when she first began supervising the school for deaf children, she was chastised and even shunned by some friends and family members who were concerned that the deaf students might pollute her (and, via their interactions with her, them). Likewise, throughout my fieldwork I participated in NSL classes, held at the associations of Deaf persons. Among my classmates were hearing Nepalis who had chosen to study NSL either to improve communication with a particular d/Deaf person or because they were interested in working as an interpreter. These classmates often commented on the social pressure against learning NSL they experienced from older relatives who cited concerns about ritual pollution.

The consequences of the association between d/Deafness and ritual pollution were, of course, typically far more severe for d/Deaf people themselves than for the hearing people with whom they interacted. For example, as mentioned in chapter 1, I was asked by the urban associations of Deaf persons to maintain a record of the deaf people I encountered when traveling in rural areas, so that representatives from these associations might later attempt to contact them and offer them support. I was warned by members of the association of Deaf people, and indeed observed on my

---

13. This is not to say that d/Deaf-hearing interactions did not occur. d/Deaf people were largely embedded in hearing networks and necessarily interacted with hearing people daily. My point is, rather, to stress that in some settings hearing Nepalis were deeply concerned about the consequences of such interactions.

travels, that it could be difficult to locate deaf individuals. Not only did I face the terminological issues outlined previously, but deaf villagers were also often tasked with work, such as herding livestock or gathering wood, which would keep them away from village or family centers for much of each day, minimizing their exposure to others. Conversely, in some cases deaf children were hidden within the home to likewise minimize exposing them to others. Deaf friends who had themselves traveled through rural areas in search of deaf villagers relayed horrible stories about encountering deaf people chained up with livestock, neglected and malnourished. In urban areas such isolation was generally less extreme. However, as Shakya's drawings in the previous chapter illustrated, revealing d/Deafness in public spaces was often highly stigmatized.

However, by the 1990s Deaf Nepalis were increasingly engaging in public displays of Deafness. For example, on an autumn morning in 2004, I drove to Kathmandu's Durbar Square to join a large gathering of members of the Kathmandu Association of the Deaf. *Darbār* means "palace," and although the seat of state power in Nepal had been moved to the nearby Narayanhiti Durbar, Durbar Square's many palaces and temples remained a prominent attraction for Nepalis and tourists. While this meeting spot had been chosen partly for its central location, the choice of a place filled with symbolic representations of the state was not incidental: We were preparing to participate in a rally for the United Nation's International Day of Persons with Disabilities, through which representatives from different groups with disabilities in Nepal sought to direct state attention to the inequalities they faced.

This event had been observed since 1992, each year highlighting a different theme. I participated for the first time in 1997, the year of "Arts, Sports, and Disabilities." I marched with the members of the Lumbini Association of the Deaf through their small town near the border with India. I was underdressed on that occasion. My one nice *kurtā salwar* (a long tunic and pants set popular with women in Nepal), was dirty, so I wore a poor substitute: a Western dress over pajama pants (while the salwar, or pants, of a kurtā salwar set are often glossed in English as "pajama pants," it is really not the same, especially when your pajama pants are plaid flannel and do not match your dress). Even though I had deemed my outfit appropriate, if not attractive, I was mortified when I arrived and realized that I would be parading through town in mismatched clothes, surrounded by friends in their finest attire.

With that experience in mind, I had purchased a ready-made kurtā salwar in flashy turquoise and gold for the 2004 event, only to arrive and find that the march was, sartorially at least, a less formal affair in Kathmandu. My friends' casual outfits complemented the baseball hats and large buttons (labeled with the name of the event and the year's theme, "Nothing About Us, Without Us"), which the association's leaders distributed for the marchers to wear. However, the members of one group of participants were dressed in formal clothing (and not asked to wear the baseball hats): the contingent from the Skill Training Institute for the Deaf (often referred to as the Swedish Sewing Project due to its primary funders), a dormitory in Kathmandu that hosted young d/Deaf women from rural areas and provided them with training in NSL, Nepali literacy, and tailoring skills. While going about their daily business at the sewing project, the women typically wore plain cotton kurtā salwar outfits, but today, in order to highlight the diverse geographical origins of the sewing project participants, many of the girls were dressed in formal clothing that signified the particular ethnic group they had been born into. One young Sherpa woman was wearing a long-sleeved dress called a *tongok,* over which she wore a colorful, striped wool *pangi* (apron), and a Gurung woman had on a dress called a *fariya* underneath her decorative *ghalek* (upper garments).

At noon we lined up and began marching through some of Kathmandu's densest neighborhoods. The marchers, in essence, demanded that onlookers notice that they were deaf. This pointed visibility was a challenge to the stigma that was associated not only with deaf people but also with the other jāts represented that day, including groups of blind marchers, as well as those with physical and developmental disabilities. However, karmic and medical disability models for understanding the nature of deafness were not the only salient perspectives raised by the Deaf marchers: Many of the banners they carried pronounced that "Nepali Sign Language is the mother tongue of Deaf people," explicitly invoking an ethnolinguistic framework for understanding Deafness.

This perspective had emerged from and helped to solidify the social, financial, and ideological relationships between the Nepali associations of Deaf persons and a range of international associations of Deaf persons that likewise promoted such a view of Deafness (including the National Association of the Hearing Impaired in Denmark [LBH], the Danish Hard of Hearing Federation, the Swedish Association of the Deaf, the Norwegian Association of the Deaf, and Britain's Deafway, among others). Deaf representatives of these institutions frequently visited Nepal to assist with local projects such as the production of NSL dictionaries, while representatives from the Nepali associations of Deaf people occasionally visited Scandinavian and British associations to observe their activities. In 1996 Nepal's NFDH (now NDFN) became a member of the World Federation of Deaf (WFD) and from that time on sent representatives to the WFD meetings, where d/Deaf people from around the world gathered. Nepali associations of Deaf people had joined the global networks of d/Deaf persons, many of which maintained that Deaf signers constituted ethnolinguistic minority groups.

Because ethnicity is often popularly understood to entail shared and essential biological, cultural, and linguistic qualities, those working to promote such a view of Deaf people have often done so in ways that advanced that perspective. In the United States a number of Deaf activists have claimed that heredity, or descent, plays a role in the constitution of Deaf ethnicity. This is most obvious in cases in which Deaf children are born to Deaf parents for genetic reasons, and, indeed, in some points of view, only Deaf (or hearing) children of Deaf parents can be considered ethnically Deaf. However, such an outlook is not universally accepted. For example, Douglas Baynton (2008) argues that ethnicity is a misleading model for describing deaf social identity precisely because it obscures the fact that most deaf children are born to hearing parents. (In the United States, some studies have shown that fewer than 5 percent of deaf children were born to deaf parents [e.g., Mitchell and Karchmer 2004].) Others have argued that, regardless of the way in which hearing loss is acquired, the condition constitutes a shared biological trait that becomes part of the basis for kinship, shared identification, and often intermarriage for those who enter Deaf social networks (e.g., Johnson and Erting 1989).

Moving away from a focus on biology, some Deaf activists in the United States have argued that Deaf communities should be viewed as ethnic rather than having a disability because they are characterized by shared norms, values, customs, languages, and artistic traditions, often acquired in social settings such as residential schools for d/Deaf students (e.g., ibid.; Lane 2005). Some promoting this perspective argue that positioning the "Deaf-World" as ethnic has positive and practical consequences for the ways in which Deaf people perceive themselves and are seen by others. In particular, this approach encourages Deaf people to "learn their language, defend their heritage against more powerful groups, study their ethnic history, and so on" (ibid., 295). In addition to these group-internal benefits, if viewed as marginalized ethnolinguistic groups, the "Deaf-World should enjoy the rights and protections accorded other ethnic groups under international law and treaties, such as the United Nations Declaration of the Rights of Persons Belonging to National or Ethnic, Religious and Linguistic Minorities" (ibid., 295).

As the frequent use of the term "ethnolinguistic" to describe this group suggests, Deaf activists have often pointed to shared language as a primary justification for an ethnic understanding of Deafness. Deaf Nepalis had adopted this transnational discourse. At the same time, however, the phrase that most commonly appeared on banners in the 2004 march, "Nepali Sign Language is the mother tongue of Deaf Nepalis," had particular salience locally, as Nepali ethnic groups such as the ādivāsi janajātis were often popularly identified and defined by their claim of a particular mother tongue other than Nepali. As mentioned earlier, the period in which Deaf Nepalis began to promote this view of Deafness was a time of war, in which a clash between Hindu nationalism and the rights of the ādivāsi janajāti and other marginalized ethnic groups was a major point of political contention. Though associations of Deaf persons had been established throughout the country, the largest and most active were in areas such as Kathmandu or Pokhara, which were controlled by the monarchy during the war. Potential alignment with other marginalized and politically active ethnolinguistic minorities in Nepal risked exposing Deaf Nepalis to the governmental discrimination, suspicion, and oppression that such groups often experienced. How did the associations of Deaf people navigate these local concerns in adopting an international model of deafness as ethnolinguistic?

On another level, how did Deaf Nepalis navigate familial concerns that sometimes arose as a result of their adoption of a Deaf ethnolinguistic identity? Most Deaf Nepalis were born into hearing households whose members did not learn NSL. Thus they were claiming as mother tongue a language that most Deaf Nepalis would never see their mothers use. How was identification with a Deaf ethnicity complicated by other ethnically based networks of belonging, such as the ādivāsi janajāti identities marked by the clothing worn by the women from the sewing project? As the next chapter shows, language policies and practices were a primary means of reflecting and affecting these complexities.

3

"My Mother Doesn't Look Like That": Nepali Sign Language as Mother Tongue

On a Friday afternoon in May 2005, two NSL teachers, named Amita and Ramesh, led a workshop for a large gathering of the members of the KAD. The purpose of the meeting was to discuss the etymology, or origins, of a group of lexical items collected in the NSL dictionary. The leaders performed a series of signs and then asked those present to explain how the signs' forms related to their meanings (the assumption was that such relationships explained the historical emergence of the sign). For example, Amita and Ramesh in turn performed each NSL sign for the months of the year (based on the Hindu Vikram Sambat calendar) and asked the members to identify a motivating relationship between the signs and the months they signified. In many cases, the group easily agreed on the nature of this relationship. For example, they collectively asserted that ASĀR (see figure 6) was motivated by the way the motion of the sign resembled the act of planting, as seeds were commonly sown in that month.

Such associations between linguistic forms and their meanings are mediated by socially situated interpretation (Bucholtz and Hall 2004). For example, in chapter 1 I explained that my Oberlin College students' perceptions of associations between speakers' ways of using language and their social identities depended on the students' own backgrounds. These associations are called indexical when they emerge from a belief that certain ways of speaking point to, or *co-occur* with, particular regions or types of persons. But associations among language use and social qualities can also be based on perceptions of iconicity. Iconicity is a relationship of resemblance or similarity between a sign and that which it represents (for example, a photograph is taken to represent a person via the image's resemblance to that person).

Although it is often assumed that iconicity is natural, essential, and therefore universal, perceptions of similarity are socially mediated. The persistent

असार / आषाढ
ASAR/AASHADH
(3rd month of year)

Figure 6

myth of a single universal sign language may in fact be in part attributed to the incorrect assumption that iconicity is always transparent. Sign languages often draw on visual resemblances between the forms of signs and their meanings; however, such associations are not universal but emerge in particular social and historical circumstances. To help my students at Oberlin College understand this contingency, I typically show them the NSL sign MOTHER, which takes the form of a bent index finger at the side of the nose (followed by the finger being laid near the side of the mouth— see figure 7). When I ask them how this sign form resembles its referent, "mother," many are baffled and see no connection. However, students in class who are from, have families from, or have spent time in South Asia are

आमा / माता
Mother

Figure 7

शुक्रबार
Friday

Figure 8

often aware of an indexical connection (co-occurrence) between nose rings (or nose studs) and women in the region. Consequently, these students are primed to perceive iconicity (resemblance) between the form of the sign and nose jewelry.[14] As these examples illustrate, when and how people perceive iconic or indexical connections between forms, things, actions, or concepts depends on their particular social histories (Irvine 2005).

Indeed, returning to the etymology workshop at the KAD, because members' interpretations of iconic and/or indexical connections between the forms of signs and their meanings were based on members' varied personal histories, the crowd did not always agree on a single interpretation of a given sign's etymology. When more than one interpretation was suggested, the leaders of the session typically declared that one or the other was correct and encouraged other participants to adopt that rationale for

---

14. Iconicity is not restricted to signed languages; people also perceive presupposed characteristics of resemblance among ways of speaking and social qualities. For example, if I play clips of speakers from different regions of the Midwest of the United States for my students, some feel that the speakers sound "the same." Some further suggest that what they perceive as a "friendly" way of speaking is due an essential quality of "friendliness" in the nature of the speakers. However, other students (often those with more experience in parts of the country considered the Midwest) perceive distinctly different accents among the clips that sound so similar to some of their classmates. They may also contest the notion that language and speakers in the region share a uniform quality of friendliness.

बोलाउनु
Call

Figure 9

the origin of the sign. In this respect, the workshop leaders validated certain interpretations (and hence backgrounds) rather than others.

For example, why, Ramesh asked the crowd, did FRIDAY take the form of the right hand held next to the face, thumb touching the cheek, with fingers outstretched and wiggling? Several people volunteered suggestions that Amita and Ramesh rejected. Then Ramesh supplied the answer that the KAD considered correct: The form of the sign FRIDAY was motivated by its similarity to the sign CALL. Both signs were located near the mouth and involved fingers moving toward the palm (see figures 8 and 9). Thus, to Ramesh, aspects of these two signs looked similar to one another.[15] He then mapped this similarity in the signs' forms onto a potential relationship between their meanings, explaining that it was on Fridays that the greatest number of members came to the KAD to socialize. Thus, on "Friday" they were "called" together.

Indeed, Friday afternoons were always the busiest days at the associations of Deaf persons in Kathmandu. Throughout the week, those members who were unemployed spent their days there, chatting and

---

15. As this suggests, iconic relationships can be perceived between elements in a linguistic system, not just between linguistic forms and their meanings. Consider the fact that English has "constellations of words in which a similarity of form evokes a similarity of meaning, such as the 'sl words' (slip, slide, slush, sleaze, etc.)" (Mannheim 1999, 107).

कृष्ण
* KRISHNA

Figure 10

participating in sign language lessons, playing board games, and helping with association projects (such as making banners or buttons for upcoming celebrations or Deaf pride marches). Those employed by these associations were also daily fixtures, making tea, preparing for teaching stints in remote villages, and/or planning and working on future and ongoing projects. Those Deaf members who were elsewhere employed, who lived on the outskirts of the Kathmandu Valley, or who were still enrolled in the schools for deaf students, however, were not able to socialize there every day. But on Friday afternoons, at a time when many were able to leave work early, almost every member was there. On such days, all of the seats that ringed the main social rooms were filled, and people spilled out into the courtyard, stood next to the busy street, and filled the surrounding *chiyā pasals* (tea shops). The relationship Ramesh perceived between the meanings of FRIDAY and CALL therefore highlighted a central feature of Deaf life in Kathmandu, the social significance of Fridays, the day of the week when most Deaf members were called, or summoned, to participate in cultural activities.

However, before the leaders of the workshop could ask about a different sign, Prabhu, another member, mentioned that he believed that FRIDAY was motivated by the sign's resemblance to the sign for the god Krishna, which represented the flute the god is often portrayed as playing (see figure 10). Though the hand is placed near a different location on the face in performing each sign, to Prabhu KRISHNA resembled FRIDAY in the shape of the hand and movement of the fingers. Although all other suggestions had been routinely rejected, at this claim Amita and Ramesh paused, conferred, and finally agreed to count this interpretation as an appropriate alternative to the previously approved etymological interpretation based on a relationship to the sign CALL. Why were the KAD leaders interested in soliciting and then unifying members' interpretations of the signs' etymologies? And why did they make an exception in this case?

As explained earlier, the adoption of an ethnolinguistic model of Deafness had the potential to align Deaf Nepalis with politically active ethnic groups during a period of intense civil strife in Nepal. Indeed, just as the state forbade the establishment of ethnic associations prior to 1990, the Kathmandu Association of the Deaf did not receive approval from the government when it was initially formed in 1980 but had to operate secretly until after the Jāna Āndolan 1. As the largest and most active associations of Deaf persons were established in areas of the country controlled by the Hindu nationalist government, the local adoption of this transnational model was thus potentially perilous. However, by encouraging members to sign in particular ways and persuading both signers and onlookers to interpret the social significance of the signs in particular ways, Deaf leaders worked to forge associations between NSL and Hindu nationalism in Nepal. This served to disrupt the alignment of Deaf Nepalis with politically active ādivāsi janajāti groups, increasing the likelihood of state support—or at least decreasing the risk of active state opposition—of Deaf sociality and advocacy during this very tense political period. Working to associate the language, and thereby Deaf Nepalis, with nationalism also served to contest the widespread association between d/Deafness and ritual pollution, which had so negatively affected d/Deaf lives. However, given the pervasiveness and strength of the stigma of deafness, how did the communicative practices that came to be labeled Nepali Sign Language arise in the first place?

The Emergence of Nepali Sign Language

As already mentioned, the Ranas (hereditary prime ministers) took control of Nepal in 1846. From that time on, they maintained a strict isolationist policy, preventing most foreign nationals from entering the country. When they were unseated in 1951, King Tribhuvan Shah opened the country to foreign visitors and investments, and tourism became a major industry in Nepal. Additionally, as a "Third World" nation without any history of colonization, Nepal became a testing ground for international aid projects enacting different ideological conceptions of "progress" and "development" (Liechty 2003, 48). A wide range of governmental (e.g., the U.S. Peace Corps) and nongovernmental organizations (NGOs) was established to channel and deploy these funds. The Shrestha family (mentioned in chapter 2) had proudly noted that they had hosted a member of the first cohort of Peace Corps volunteers in the country. The family went on to house an almost unbroken chain of foreigners, including additional Peace Corps members, volunteers from various NGOs, and study-abroad students such as me. Their photo albums and address books provide a microcosmic view of the proliferation of such institutions in Nepal.

Several of the aid programs that emerged during this period oversaw projects specifically related to deafness, including but not limited to the Peace Corps, the Britain Nepal Otology Service, the Swedish Organizations of Persons with Disabilities International Development Cooperation Association (SHIA), and Nepal's Welfare Society for the Hearing Impaired (WSHI). Some worked to prevent, diagnose, and treat hearing loss, while others provided educational resources for deaf children whose hearing could not be sufficiently restored. The goal of the latter programs was typically to help deaf persons function analogously to, or ideally pass as, hearing persons in order to "cure" their deafness socially, if not physically. Consequently, their pedagogical approaches were typically oralist, focused on teaching children to read lips and produce spoken Nepali while strictly discouraging the use of gesture or signed language.

In 1966, Queen Ratna (the second wife of King Mahendra Shah, Tribhuvan's successor) worked in cooperation with Dr. Laxmi Narayan Prasad and an American Peace Corps volunteer to establish the first formal school for deaf students in the country. Initially, its classes were held in two rooms in the Bir Hospital compound in Kathmandu, but the school was subsequently expanded into a larger institution with residential capacities, the

Naxal School for the Deaf. As Kiran Acharya, one of the school's first students, wrote in his "History of the Deaf in Nepal," "the teachers working at the instruction center did not allow the deaf students to communicate or study using sign language. In order to suppress our natural tendency to communicate (with signs), the teachers would scold us, hold our hands down, twist our ears, and pull our hair" (1997, 1). However, by gathering together a critical mass of deaf children, the school created conditions for the establishment of signing practices and deaf sociality.

The teachers were not able to monitor the students' interactions at all times. "[D]uring class hours signs were not used. However, when 1:00 came, the time for *tiffin* (lunch), students could surreptitiously communicate through visual and gestural modalities. After 4:00 in the afternoon we were free to talk to each other using signs after leaving school. There was no particular reason to return home early if we did not have to, since we were not able to communicate effectively with our families. So we would gather in a specific place after school to socialize until 7:00 or 8:00 in the evening" (ibid., 4). Acharya and other leaders of Nepali associations of Deaf people suggest that NSL emerged from the communicative interactions of the first several cohorts of students in the schools for deaf students (Acharya 1997; Sharma 2003; Khanal 2013a).

It is not clear whether NSL emerged from these interactions from scratch, that is, without any influence from other previously existing sign languages, as has been claimed for the genesis of Nicaraguan Sign Language (e.g., Kegl, Senghas, and Coppola 1999). This is possible in principle. The deaf children certainly drew on their varying gestural repertoires to interactively construct a communicative code to facilitate their interactions. Each incoming cohort of students could build on these practices, adding complexity and structure, until the system became fully linguistic. However, influence from sign languages in the surrounding regions also seems likely; before schools for deaf students were established in Nepal, wealthy parents of deaf children sometimes sent their offspring to schools for deaf students in India. These children sometimes returned fluent in Indian Sign Language (Sharma 2003). Some scholars indeed argue that NSL is an offshoot of what they consider a regional Indo-Pakistani Sign Language (e.g., Zeshan 2000). Additionally, the fact that some signers from the first cohorts at the Naxal school, including Kiran Acharya, currently sign with a complexity comparable to that of later-generation signers, suggests that they may have been exposed to full-blown language earlier than the from-scratch scenario might suggest (Morgan 2013). I argue that NSL (like all languages) is not a discrete and homogeneous monolith but a complex set of overlapping and diverging communicative practices that emerged from signers' social interactions and diverse repertoires. From this perspective, all of the foregoing factors could be relevant in the development of the suite of practices currently referred to as NSL.[16]

Whatever the origins of NSL, associations of Deaf people soon became another important site for its continued development through interaction. As mentioned above, students often gathered after school to socialize using sign language. Sometimes they patronized nearby tea shops for this purpose. On other occasions they would simply stand in the street and chat. In either setting they were exposed to the scrutiny, commentary, and sometimes scorn of passersby. This exposure was beneficial, however, when some Deaf Italian tourists who happened to be visiting the country encountered deaf students socializing near the school and encouraged them to form Deaf clubs or associations, where they could privately communicate as they pleased and from which they could advocate for Deaf rights (including the right to use sign language).

In 1995, what was then called the NFDH (now NDFN) was founded in Kathmandu as an umbrella institution to organize what had become eight regional associations of Deaf Nepalis. In addition to their functions as places for socialization and advocacy, the associations collected and disseminated signs by publishing NSL dictionaries[17] and began offering NSL classes to d/Deaf people who had been unable to attend a school for deaf persons. They also began pressuring the Naxal school (and other subsequently founded

---

16. Diversity in both the origins and the current structures of NSL practice, however, should not be misunderstood as an indication that these signing practices are anything less than fully linguistic. As discussed in chapter 1, such variation characterizes human linguistic practice generally and, in fact, is a source of communicative richness.

17. The dictionary projects received funding from Denmark's LBH and Britain's Deafway.

schools for deaf students) to abandon their stringent oralist policies.[18] In 1988, in response to the associations' efforts and to broader trends in education for deaf students internationally, the principal of the Naxal school adopted the Total Communication pedagogical approach to education for deaf students, which allowed the use of sign languages in the classroom, along with other communicative resources such as speech, writing, or gesture.

However, the signed communication generally used in Total Communication classrooms took the form of manual signs mapped onto grammatical constructions derived from the dominant spoken language. This practice had a long history, going back to the Abbé Charles-Michel de l'Épée, a pioneer in education for d/Deaf persons and often referred to as the Father of the Deaf. He added French grammar to his students' signed lexical items, calling this "methodical signing." Likewise, the (almost exclusively hearing) teachers in the Nepali schools for deaf children began to perform signs derived from the dictionaries produced by the association of Deaf persons but mapped them onto Nepali spoken language grammatical patterns. In addition to being supported by the Total Communication philosophy, this practice allowed the Naxal school to claim to the government that it offered instruction in Nepali, the national language. Prior to the Jāna Āndolan 1, this was required if the school's students were to be allowed to take the School Leaving Certificate (SLC) exams, roughly equivalent to a high school diploma in the United States.

On some occasions the teachers' efforts to map NSL signs onto Nepali grammatical constructions led to misunderstandings between the teachers and the students. As an illustration, one afternoon in 2005 I was visiting Mrs. Joshi's second-grade classroom in the Naxal School for the Deaf (see transcript 1). She pointed to a drawing of a cow and asked the students, in simultaneously produced spoken and signed Nepali, "What does the cow give us?" Anil, a small boy sitting in the front of the classroom, eagerly lunged into Mrs. Joshi's field of vision and signed, "GRASS!" She furrowed her brow and asked him skeptically, "Grass from a cow?" Anil sank back into his seat. Another student, Prem, waved for her attention and signed, "MILK!" Mrs. Joshi congratulated him heartily for this correct answer. Was

---

18. The Gandaki School for the Deaf in Pokhara is notable for having offered sign language–medium instruction since its establishment.

Anil unaware that cows provide humans with milk? Or was there something about Mrs. Joshi's signing that led him to answer as he did (see transcript 1)?

Transcript 1

Teacher's Speech	Teacher's Signs	Students' Responses
1. *Yo gāile hāmi, hāmilāi ke dinchha?*	1. IS THIS WE- WE TO WHAT GIVE THIS?	
		2. GRASS
3. *Gāile le grass ho?*		
		4. MILK
5. *Shābāsh!*	5. THANK-YOU/CONGRATULATIONS!	

In fact, the latter was the more likely explanation. To explain how Anil misunderstood Mrs. Joshi, it is helpful to compare her signing with that of a Deaf teacher, Mrs. Dangol. During my research, each Baisāk (the first month of the Nepali year) a new group of adolescent d/Deaf girls recruited primarily from rural areas came to live and study at the Swedish Sewing Project. The girls, too old to enter the Naxal school, lived together for one year while learning NSL, attaining literacy in Nepal, and acquiring sewing skills. The following example is derived from one of Mrs. Dangol's language classes. She had just used the NSL sign JHĀKRI ("shaman"). Realizing that not all of her students were familiar with the term, she defined it by signing the following: "In a village, when you are sick and there are no doctors or medicine. The jhākri exorcises you, exorcises me, like this. Do you understand? You've seen this? He bangs on a drum and wears a feathered headdress" (see transcript 2).

Transcript 2

1. JHĀKRI.
   Jhākri.

2. VILLAGE YOU-PLURAL SICK MEDICAL-DOCTOR, MEDICINE ISN'T.
   In the village, when you are sick, there are no doctors or medicine.

3. JHĀKRI EXORCISES-YOU, EXORCISES-ME.
   The jhākri exorcises you, like this.

4. YOU-PLURAL UNDERSTAND?
  Do you understand?

5. SEEN? SEEN YOU-PLURAL?
  You've seen this?

In so doing, she drew on a range of grammatical strategies that took advantage of the visual modality of NSL. For example, when she signed "exorcises you," she formed her hand into the shape a jhākri's hand would take on when using a brush to fling water on a client as part of a healing ritual and moved it away from her body and toward the students. When she changed perspectives and signed, "exorcises me," she reversed this directionality and moved her hand toward her own body. This strategy of indicating meaning, such as who is acting on whom, through the movement of a verb through space was common to the way most d/Deaf children and adults performed NSL. Sign language linguists label this kind of construction an "agreeing verb" (Padden 1983).

Knowing this we can now understand Anil's confusion in response to Mrs. Joshi's question. When Mrs. Joshi asked the students what the cow gives us, in her spoken Nepali she attached to the Nepali word gāi ("cow") the Nepali suffix le, that indicates the agent of an action (i.e., gāile-: "by the cow"). She attached to the Nepali word hāmi ("us") the suffix lāi, which indicates to whom or to what an action was performed (hāmilāi: "to us"). Thus it was quite clear that she was asking what the cow gives to us rather than the other way around. But in Mrs. Joshi's signed channel this was much less clear. In signing practice that takes advantage of spatial grammatical possibilities (which most students used among themselves), GIVE would most likely move directionally from the image of the cow toward the signer's body. However, the NSL dictionary from which Mrs. Joshi had likely learned the sign represented the sign as moving away from the signer's chest (as this was the generic form; see figure 11). She may not have been aware that it was possible to modify the sign by changing the direction in which it moved. Thus, she performed GIVE moving away from her chest, and Anil, therefore, logically believing that she was asking, "What do we give the cow?" answered "Grass!"

Over time, however, students such as Anil often developed the ability to switch between these grammatical styles when talking to d/Deaf or hearing people; they incorporated multiple styles of signing into their linguistic

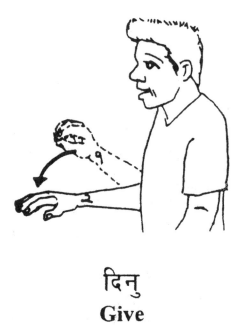

दिनु
Give

Figure 11

repertoires. For example, in 2004 I observed an NSL class in Pharphing, a small town on the edge of the Kathmandu Valley. The class was held in midmorning, after most Nepalis have had a light breakfast but before the day's first substantive meal of *dāl bhāt* (lentils, rice, and vegetables) at 10 a.m. Four d/Deaf adults (who were too old to attend the Naxal school) and two young hearing participants were present.[19] The instructor, Birendra, was a member of one of the first cohorts of students from the Naxal school and a high-ranking leader at the KAD.

The class began with Birendra asking everyone to state their names. Turning to a hearing participant, he signed YOU-POSSESIVE NAME WHAT IS? Though Birendra did not speak or mouth these words, his signs mapped perfectly onto the corresponding sentence in spoken Nepali: Tapāi-ko nām ke ho? ("What is your name?"). He then asked the same question of a Deaf

---

19. The hearing participants were interested in learning NSL in order to interact with a Deaf relative. It sometimes did, happily, occur that hearing family members tried to learn NSL; unfortunately, this was rare.

participant. In doing so, he simply signed NAME, grammatically specifying the addressee through eye gaze and signifying that he was asking a question through his brow furrow and chin lift. (In NSL, as in other sign languages that linguists have studied, facial expressions, postural shifts, and other "nonmanuals" have been incorporated into the grammar of the language; sign languages do not rely solely on the hands.) In this and other contexts, Deaf Nepalis often used Nepali-language influenced signing when addressing a hearing signer and shifted to use spatial and non-manual grammatical constructions when addressing a fellow Deaf signer.

However, despite such systematic grammatical differences in how hearing and Deaf people tended to sign, as well as grammatical differences among Deaf signers (see chapter 4), during the time of my research most people considered such signing to be the same language: NSL.[20] Indeed, the primary criterion by which signing practice was identified as NSL was whether or not it drew on the corpus of lexical items collected in the Nepali Sign Language dictionaries produced by associations of Deaf persons. NSL did not have a widely used written form; the NSL dictionaries thus consisted of pictorial representations (such as those produced by Shakya) of individual lexical items linked to glosses in Nepali and English. The fact that there was no means of representing the grammatical structures of NSL in print encouraged an exclusive focus on lexical items in both the dictionaries and the local language ideologies among Deaf Nepalis.

Standardizing NSL

The sociopolitical context in which Deaf Nepalis adopted an ethnolinguistic model of Deafness was dominated by a linguistic monolith perspective on the nature of language. Indeed, the very name—Nepali Sign Language—implied a language uniform within and coincident with the borders of the Nepali nation-state. This ideological perspective is often accompanied by what is sometimes called a "monoglot standard" language ideology (Silverstein 1996). This is the widespread belief, unsupported

---

20. Green (2014) notes that, during her research in Nepal in 2010, Deaf Nepalis explicitly labeled these styles "short" and "long" signing. That is, although both forms were still ideologically identified as NSL, the differences between them were becoming subject to more explicit, as well as implicit, distinction.

by linguistic research, that, when multiple variants of a linguistic form exist, only one can be correct. Standardization projects may therefore be undertaken to reduce optional variation in language use (Milroy and Milroy 1999). Indeed, such a project was among the explicit goals of Nepal's associations of Deaf persons. For example, in the introduction to the NSL dictionary (2003, viii), the NFDH (now NDFN) stated its goal to "make one Nepali Sign Language which is accepted by all and bring it into use," while in the "History of the Deaf in Nepal" (Acharya 1997, 6) suggested that the "possibility that the diversity of the signs will expand" was a "danger."

The historical process of standardization typically involves the selection of a particular variety of a language, the establishment of strict norms for its use, the elaboration of its adoption in various sociolinguistic domains, and public acceptance of its claim to "correctness" (Haugen 1996). The associations of Deaf people considered this process their provenance, stating in the introduction to the NSL dictionary that if "any person or organization collects, establishes or develops new signs, they are to be presented before the Nepali Sign Language National Development committee (made up of representatives from the Deaf association leadership). Only those signs that are ratified according to rules by the Nepali Sign Language National Development committee will be recognized as standard" (2003, viii).

Standardization projects generally focus on reducing variation in only a particular set of linguistic features (out of the many levels of complexity that characterize language use). Although the standardization of English in the United States, for instance, has focused primarily on reducing variation in lexical and grammatical structures, in the United Kingdom the process has concentrated more on phonological features such as accent (Milroy and Milroy 1999). Because lexical items were the primary basis for identifying signing as NSL, standardization efforts led by the association of Deaf people focused on reducing variation at this level, while grammatical variation such as that described earlier was not subject to these processes.

Moreover, although the ultimate goal of language standardization is purportedly the reduction of variation in linguistic practice, actually reducing such variation may be less important than the social indexicalities that motivate the process and provide frameworks for interpreting its results (ibid.). That is, the choice of forms to designate as standard often has more to do with the social status of the speakers associated with them than with any linguistic feature per se. Further, standardization projects do not simply reflect social relationships but, by seeking to transform how people use and interpret the significance of language, can also influence or even produce particular types of social relations (i.e., if a language variety comes to be designated as "standard" or "nonstandard," what does that imply about its users?).

As an illustration, varieties of English that were considered standard in the United States both reflected and produced a notion of the standard speaker as middle class, mainstream, and racially unmarked, whereas in the United Kingdom the standard forms both reflected and produced elite, high-class status (ibid.). Likewise, the project to standardize NSL involved efforts to reduce variation not only in the ways people signed but also in the social information people derived from these forms. Specifically, the project to standardize NSL aimed to link the language, and thereby a Deaf ethnolinguistic identity, with symbols of the Nepali nation (and hence with symbols of caste Hinduism). Because these associations ran counter to popular beliefs about d/Deafness, these efforts pushed against the grain. Thus, this standardization project sought to produce, rather than reflect, a social category by creating new indexical connections between language and Deafness.

In this respect, the standardization project could be characterized as a form of sanskritization, a process by which a group seeks to raise its status by adopting practices associated with higher castes (Srinivas 1967, 67–82). (The term is derived from the word "Sanskrit," the name of the language in which many canonical Hindu texts were written.) Given the long dominance of caste Hindu perspectives in Nepal, this was a fairly common historical process. For example, a number of leaders of the Thakali jāt, who had been defined as matwāli in the *Muluki Ain*, enacted proscriptions against non-Hindu practices such as eating yak meat, drinking brewed alcohol, or wearing Tibetan-style clothing. Thus, some anthropologists characterized the Thakali as a people who "purposefully and unilaterally" changed their cultural practices to raise their social status in a Hindu-dominated society (Fürer-Haimendorf 1978, 6). Other scholars noted that this shift did not characterize the practices of all those who identified themselves as Thakali, however, and since the 1990s, many politically active Thakalis have worked to revive practices that had been previously downplayed (Fisher 2001).

How did Deaf leaders try to reconstruct the indexical connotations of NSL and Deafness? One way, of course, was to select as standard and enshrine in the NSL dictionaries those signs that could have potential links to caste Hinduism and Nepali nationalism. But such associations are not inherent. As the opening discussion of the KAD etymology workshop showed, signers might interpret the motivations for and indexical associations of standard signs in different ways. Thus one reason for holding such workshops was to standardize not only the way people produced signs but also the ways in which they interpreted them. And that is likely why an indexical link to the god Krishna was accepted as an approved interpretation of the motivation for the form of FRIDAY. Not only did the invocation of a Hindu god align with caste Hinduism and nationalist sentiment, but it also drew on an analogue with spoken Nepali, the national language, in the following ways:

The Nepali language names for the days of the week—Sombār (Monday), Maṇgalbār (Tuesday), Budhabār (Wednesday), Bihibār (Thursday), Śukrabār (Friday), Sanibār (Saturday), and Āitabār (Sunday)—are made up of the name of a deity, followed by *bār* ("day"). This is because, according to Hindu astrology, a particular deity is associated with each day of the week. Most of the standard NSL signs for the days of the week could be linked to these Nepali words through varying, and sometimes quite complicated, connections. Consider this illustration: MONDAY is related to the word "Sombār" through its use of initialization. The handshape for the sign is that used in the local fingerspelling system, which is based on the Devanagari script, and represents the first letter in the written Nepali word. In addition, TUESDAY resembled the trunk of an elephant and, in so doing, invoked Ganesh, a Hindu god with the head of an elephant. This was because, though Maṇgal in Maṇgalbār refers to a different god, Ganesh is often referred to as *mangal mūrti* ("auspicious deity"). In this case, the relationship of the form of the sign to Ganesh was mediated by the similarity of the two spoken Nepali words. For such links to be salient, signers had to have access to Nepali (and most did, though Deaf Nepalis had different levels of access to the language, as literacy levels, residual hearing, and degree of oralist training varied greatly among association members). Like the other Nepali words mentioned earlier, the word for

Friday, Śukrabār, was derived from the name of the Hindu god Śukra, a teacher of the *asuras* (or antigods). Otherwise no direct connection existed between Śukra and Krishna. Prabhu's suggestion was based on a similarity between the standard forms of FRIDAY and KRISHNA, aligned with the general Nepali language pattern of linking days of the week and Hindu gods.

With regard to kinship terms, the NSL signs that were chosen as standard were those that potentially indexed caste Hinduism. As mentioned earlier, the standard form of MOTHER in NSL was produced by first placing a bent finger at the side of the nose (indicating female-ness generally) and then placing the finger alongside the mouth (indicating, specifically, parental status). Those who compiled the dictionary understood the sign as resembling a nose ring or stud, which could in turn index those social groups in which women wore this style of jewelry (including caste Hindus but excluding, for example, Newars and Sherpas, two major ethnic groups in Nepal). As a result, in addition to denoting the concept "mother," this sign could have Hindu connotations. This form could in turn be treated as emblematic of Deaf Nepalis as a social group, suggesting that they were (or resembled) caste Hindus.

Some signers readily noticed this connotation. For example, one afternoon Anu, a young Deaf woman who lived on the outskirts of the Kathmandu Valley, invited me to lunch. After we ate, we took a walk through some fields of mustard greens near her house. As we crested a small hill, she pointed to a nearby settlement and signed to me that its inhabitants were "dirty" and "poor." Herself an upper-caste Hindu, she then attempted to indicate that the settlement was inhabited by a social group other than her own. It was a Newar neighborhood (the Newar ethnic group has an internal caste system, with high and low groups, associated with varying degrees of ritual purity). Not knowing the standard sign for Newar, she repeatedly signed that nose jewelry was not worn there, while indicating her own nose stud. Because she lived in proximity to this Newar village, she was able to observe the social distinctions marked by symbols such as jewelry, spatial segregation (close but visibly separate villages), and differing house form and to imbibe local attitudes regarding these differences.

However, many Deaf signers came from social groups, such as the Newars or the Sherpas, which did not permit women to pierce their noses. Such signers did not always automatically associate MOTHER in NSL with nose rings. Without explicit instruction, some assumed that the sign

आमा

MOTHER

Figure 12

simply pointed to the nose and furnished explanations of the association between the form and its referent that made sense to them, given their experiences. For example, d/Deaf children sometimes interpreted the sign form as indicating "snot" and rationalized the form of the sign as motivated by the fact that a mother might wipe her child's nose. In the case at hand, to make such links more salient to members of the associations of Deaf persons and students in the schools for d/Deaf children, Pratigya Shakya, the Deaf Nepali artist whose work we saw in chapter 1 and who also illustrated the NSL dictionaries, created a series of posters that visually encoded these institutions' approved understandings of the motivations underlying the standard sign forms.

For example, his illustration of MOTHER (shown in figure 12) depicted a Hindu woman both performing and embodying the sign. This social identity was indicated by her clothing (i.e., a bright red blouse rather than the maroon associated with rural Buddhist ethnic groups). This imagery further narrowed the connotation of the sign, excluding ethnic groups such as the Rai, in which nose jewelry is worn. The elaboration of the caste-Hindu association in the poster, through the depiction of the mother's clothing, was one of the ways the standardization project attempted to direct attention to an indexical link between the linguistic form and a particular social meaning.

Because these associations ran counter to popular beliefs about d/Deafness, this project was an effort to use social indexicality to produce a new social category rather than simply reflecting and reproducing an existing one. How successful was this reframing? The associations of Deaf persons did not have the power to completely reverse indexical links between d/Deafness and pollution for the entire population of Nepal. However, these efforts registered their rejection of this framing. Furthermore, linking NSL to symbols of nationalism arguably did influence state reception of Deaf identity work: Although support was always scanty, actual opposition ceased. However, how did these efforts affect Deaf Nepalis born into noncaste Hindu families, including ādivāsi janajātis, Dalits, and Madhesis, many of whom were pointedly excluded by such standard connotations?

Mother Tongue and Mothers

Because the causes of deafness were not typically genetic, d/Deaf Nepalis were overwhelmingly born into hearing families. In some cases relations with family members could be strained or even broken off due to the stigma of d/Deafness. Though this was not always the case, and many d/Deaf Nepalis remained integrated into their family networks to varying degrees, it was exceedingly rare for hearing family members to learn NSL. That is not to say that d/Deaf and hearing family members did not communicate with each other. In most cases d/Deaf Nepalis and their daily interlocutors constructed idiosyncratic gestural systems, which d/Deaf Nepalis called "natural signs." These systems varied widely in complexity, from extremely rudimentary to languagelike, depending on the quality and quantity of communicative interactions between a d/Deaf person and that person's family or social network. Natural signs, or as they are typically referred to in the literature, homesigns, were often grounded in the particularities of a given household, reflecting personal histories, characteristics, and relationships. They were not typically considered alternative sign languages. For example, in 2004 I conducted a survey in which I asked members of the KAD to list the languages they used. On a few occasions members started to list natural signs but were instructed by onlookers that these "did not count" as language.

The contrast between homesigns and the standard NSL lexicon was another way in which the standard forms' intended iconic and indexical links to upper-caste Hindu practices and Hindu nationalism in Nepal could become clear to signers. For example, a Deaf Sherpa child from the Solo Khumbu region, who studied in an urban school for d/Deaf students, had not been aware that MOTHER could connote "Hindu-ness" (Taylor 1997). He became aware of this link only after having returned home for a visit, when his attempts to use the sign in reference to his actual mother, instead of their previously constructed homesign, caused affront to the family, to whom the link was quite salient. The standard connotations could offend because, though concurrent belonging to different jāts was to be expected (e.g., a given person might typically belong simultaneously to both a caste jāt and a gendered jāt), some jāt categories were seen as more or less mutually exclusive: Caste and ethnic jāt identities often fell into this category.

Thus homesigns and the noncaste Hindu birth identities they sometimes indicated became a foil against which standard NSL and a Deaf jāt were defined. Accordingly, standardization efforts in the associations of Deaf people worked to narrow not only the indexical associations of standard signs but also those derived from the homesigns identified as nonstandard signing. For example, sign language teachers frequently described common homesigns for "mother," often related to breasts (as in nursing) or hairstyles, as sexual, vulgar, and inappropriate. Many Deaf Nepalis navigated this potential conflict between NSL and homesigns by compartmentalizing their signing practices, using standard NSL signs at the associations of Deaf persons but continuing to use homesigns with family members. As my friend Ramachandra pointed out one afternoon in 2004, the embarrassment of revealing their particular homesign systems to their signing friends sometimes discouraged Deaf Nepalis from inviting other Deaf signers to their homes. Indeed, Ramachandra felt the need to give me a disclaimer about the homesigns I would witness him use with his family that afternoon. Other Deaf friends felt less anxiety about the need to modify their signing practices to suit the context.

Such practices might suggest that NSL and Deaf sociality were located outside family networks, grounded solely in institutional settings such as schools or associations of Deaf persons. However, people produce kinship ties through marriage as well as birth. The first cohorts of NSL users graduating from the schools for d/Deaf students typically married hearing Nepalis from the appropriate birth jāt, chosen by their parents, as was largely the norm in Nepal.[21] Although some of these marriages yielded satisfactory

21. However, the methods by which marriage partners were chosen varied according to jāt and region.

relationships, many Deaf Nepalis complained that marriage to a hearing partner who did not learn NSL was alienating. While male signers could continue to come to the associations of Deaf persons for NSL-mediated sociality after marriage, female signers were typically more restricted to the home and lost access to settings in which NSL might be used.

Subsequent cohorts of Deaf Nepalis increasingly prioritized marriage within Deaf signing networks. In some cases this led to marriages between Deaf partners of different birth jāts who would not typically be considered appropriate marriage partners. For example, Tinley and Geeta, a Deaf couple with whom I became good friends in 1997, met while attending the residential school for d/Deaf students in Pokhara. Tinley was born into an ethnically Thakali family, while Geeta was born into a caste Hindu family from the Terai. They married without approval from their families. As a consequence, they were firmly expelled from both of their birth social groups. After marriage they remained in Pokhara rather than relocate to Tinley's village, as would have been expected under usual circumstances, and allowed the Deaf social networks there to replace the kinship networks they had lost. As another illustration, Roshika and Dhanu, born into Newar and Gurung families, respectively, also married without the approval of their families. I was visiting at the KAD one afternoon in 2004 when they stopped in to share the news that they had eloped and were moving to Pokhara together, where they, too, would draw on existing Deaf social networks to establish themselves. They were feted and applauded by the KAD members.

In some cases, when a hearing family would not facilitate a marriage between Deaf Nepalis, the leaders of an association of Deaf people would (often with some reluctance) step in as proxies for the parents. For example, Maya, a young Deaf woman from a remote region in western Nepal, spent a year in Kathmandu with the sewing project. Upon completing the program she did not want to return to her birth village, where no one signed. She decided instead to elope with a young Deaf man. However, he robbed and abandoned her in the city, at which point she came to the KAD for assistance. The leaders were deeply concerned about her situation. Although they did not want to return her to her home unmarried, where she would be subject to intense shaming, they did not feel they could personally take on the responsibility of supporting her in the city. Finally, they decided to assist her by locating a suitable marriage partner in Kathmandu. They nominated Bibek, a bachelor who was gainfully employed as an electrician. While not of the exact caste background as Maya, the match was close enough—and acceptable to his family, with whom the couple would ideally reside. Bibek was not entirely sure that he wanted to get married but was willing to consider the possibility when approached by the leaders of the KAD. Typically, a young man's parents would first show him a photograph of a prospective bride and then arrange a formal meeting if he wanted to proceed. In this case, as the leaders of the KAD lacked a photograph of Maya, I was recruited to briefly film her and then (with her permission) show the footage to the potential groom.

Several days after this viewing, a formal meeting was arranged, and I was invited to attend as, by helping with the previewing by videotaping Maya, I had been drawn into the matchmaking process. The KAD was filled with onlookers, excited that a Deaf marriage was potentially in the making. For privacy, the couple, Roshan (then the president of the association), Manju (a female Deaf teacher), and I adjourned to the president's office and shut the door. The would-be bride and groom were extremely nervous and declined to sign directly to one another. In fact, the only explicit comment either one made about the other was Maya's slightly panicked comment to Manju, "He looks old!" Bibek did not respond to this remark or offer any of his own. This event paralleled a typical engagement procedure in most ways, except for the fact that the leaders of the association performed the role normally reserved for the woman's parents. However, the hearing families were not cut completely out of the process: The groom's family was consulted first, and, after the viewing was completed, a member of the association escorted the Deaf women back to her home village, where the proposed marriage was presented to her family for their approval.

In the majority of cases the potential tension in prioritizing Deaf or birth jāt in a marriage partner was resolved by the hearing family members' agreeing to find a Deaf marriage partner from a compatible birth caste or ethnicity. For example, my friend Kamal insisted to his family that he would marry only another d/Deaf person; however, not having any particular individual in mind, he allowed them to scour their own networks for a deaf woman of the appropriate Newar caste. They were able to find a few suitable d/Deaf girls from the correct social group, and he chose Sunita from among them. As a result, the couple remained within the joint family system, living in Kamal's ancestral home.

When a Deaf couple who were accustomed to using NSL together in associations of Deaf people and schools married, NSL was introduced into family spaces. However, the married couples I knew reported (and I observed this when visiting their homes) that, while they used NSL when communicating with one another at home, they continued to shift to homesigns when addressing hearing family members, including their own hearing children. This entailed the marriage partners' becoming familiar with the homesign systems used by their in-laws. In some cases, signers who had been socialized by authoritative figures in the institutions for Deaf people to view certain types of homesigns as vulgar took it upon themselves to put an end to the use of these by their in-laws. For instance, on one occasion in 2005, Jitendra, a close friend, while introducing me to his Deaf wife's hearing family (they were both born into marriage-compatible Newar castes), took me aside and proudly explained that he had stamped out the use of nonstandard kinship signs within their household. Regarding the homesign his wife had used to refer to her mother, he signed the following:

> She had a sign of her own that she understood. Her sign was different from the standard sign for "mother." It was the same as women have . . . I'm ashamed to say. Maybe you'll see me making this sign and be surprised. Here, in Nepali culture . . . The sign was like, um, the same as milk. I'm scared to say it. Do you understand? Breasts! It was like breasts! . . . I saw this and told her OK, this is wrong. In the past she had no language. Now she has switched. I told her the nonstandard sign for "mother" was not good. I told her the standard sign MOTHER, MOTHER, MOTHER is better.

When Jitendra had learned that his wife's homesign for mother had been motivated by an association with nursing, he worked to convince the family that such a sign was inappropriate and that they should adopt the standard sign (despite its indicating a nose ring, which Newari women do not wear) as the more respectable alternative. The standardization project of the association of Deaf persons had managed, in this case, to convert an understanding of this homesign from one that signified "nurturing" to one that was shamefully sexual.

However, it is important to note that this standardization work focused primarily on language as the most politically salient marker of both jāt and national identity rather than on other social practices, such as dress or diet. For example, readers may recall from the previous chapter that students from the sewing project marched in the International Day of Persons with

Disabilities parade wearing clothing that signaled their ādivāsi janajāti birth jāt affiliations. Indeed, leaders of associations of Deaf persons never discouraged their members from wearing clothing or engaging in religious or social practices associated with their birth jāts. However, official association events were typically centered on Hindu national holidays. For example, each of the associations of Deaf persons in the Kathmandu Valley hosted a yearly picnic for its members in order to celebrate the Nepali New Year as reckoned by the Hindu Vikram Sambat calendar. Many association members born into ādivāsi janajāti groups also observed Lochar, a celebration of the new year as reckoned by a Chinese/Tibetan lunar calendar. While I attended Lochar celebrations at the homes of Deaf friends, such events were organized around birth—rather than Deaf—networks of belonging.

In conclusion, the project to standardize NSL entailed efforts to link a Deaf jāt to symbols of Nepali nationalism and ritual purity. On the one hand, this involved attempts to make diverse ways of using and interpreting language converge, framing NSL as a linguistic monolith onto which a likewise monolithic Deaf jāt could be mapped. But this ideological framing also required variation in how people signed, which Deaf leaders could treat as a foil against which standard forms and interpretations could emerge. This project was neither all-encompassing nor unchanging; efforts to link NSL and a Deaf jāt to Nepali nationalism and caste Hinduism were responsive to the particular historical moment of my research. As chapter 6 explains, several aspects of these social processes changed with the end of both the civil war in 2006 and the monarchy in 2008.

Nevertheless, at the time of my research, the associations of Deaf people treated homesigns that emerged in family contexts, which often reflected non-Hindu or ādivāsi janajāti practices and symbols, as a contrast against which standard NSL and its links to nationalism could emerge. However, a number of deaf Nepalis were unable to learn the standard NSL lexicon and relied solely on their homesign systems to communicate. As an ethnolinguistic framing of a Deaf jāt was grounded in use of standard NSL, how were such homesigners affected by the adoption of this perspective? Chapter 4 explores this topic.

"Here in Nepal There Are No Old Deaf People": Homesigners, Copying, and Competence

4

As CHAPTER 1 EXPLAINS, I first visited Nepal as an undergraduate. My study-abroad program culminated by requiring its students to conduct independent research projects of our own design. Because I had been taking NSL lessons throughout the semester, I decided to focus my project on Nepal's Deaf community. One afternoon near the end of my four-week project, while writing up field notes and drafting my research paper, I noticed something odd about my data. Every Deaf person I had met, spent time with, or interviewed—every NSL teacher, every leader in the associations of Deaf people, every Deaf friend who had invited me to their home, every Deaf person to whom those friends had introduced me—had been under the age of forty.

This struck me as a serious problem with my research project, which I believed should present a comprehensive picture of Nepal's Deaf community (a lofty goal for a fledgling twenty-year-old researcher with four weeks to devote to the project and, as I later came to understand, a frankly outdated notion of ethnography).[22] Determined to correct this error before the research period came to an end, I immediately left my rented room and sought out my friend Shrihari. Like me, Shrihari was then twenty years old and had been instrumental in introducing me to many of the Deaf Nepalis I had interviewed for my project. I assumed his youthful social network

22. Although earlier anthropologists strove to present comprehensive portraits of cultural groups, since the 1980s those working in the discipline have been sensitive to the ways in which such studies falsely constructed notions of cultures as bounded, discrete, and timeless. Currently, anthropologists tend to focus on cultural processes rather than cultures as products.

had skewed my data and hoped that he could quickly arrange for me to meet as many older Deaf Nepalis as possible during the last days remaining for my research. I found him socializing at the association of Deaf people and took him aside to make my urgent request. Shrihari started to laugh and, after composing himself, smiled at me with patient amusement and signed, "Here in Nepal there *are* no old Deaf people."

My readers are likely less surprised by this answer than I was. As mentioned earlier, the first school for deaf students was not established in Nepal until 1966, and NSL may not have developed until years later. The oldest Deaf Nepalis I had met, those nearing forty, were part of the first known cohort of NSL signers in Nepal. The vast majority of those born profoundly deaf beforehand had no opportunity to learn an accessible language during childhood or adolescence. A large body of literature, discussed in more detail later, argues that humans who do not acquire any language during this developmental period are often highly constrained in their ability to learn language later in life. Thus, although many nonhearing people of all ages lived in Nepal, because they were not NSL signers, those older than forty could not be considered Deaf within the ethnolinguistic framework through which Shrihari had understood my question.

Fast-forward seven years to an autumn afternoon in 2004. I was back in Nepal as a PhD candidate, now doing research on NSL and Deaf social networks for my dissertation. By this point I well understood that I should not expect to encounter older people in Deaf social life. Therefore I was very surprised when the companions with whom I was sharing tea and conversation at the NDFN looked over my shoulder at someone entering the room and excitedly signed, "The old Deaf man! He's here!" My friends explained that this man, Madhu, communicated primarily by means of "natural signs," or homesigns, idiosyncratic systems of gestural communication developed in the absence of an established language. Homesigners not exposed to full-blown language in childhood vary in their abilities to acquire language later in life, according to factors such as their age at first exposure to language and the complexity of their homesign system (Newport 1990). Because Madhu had not been exposed to sign language until he was over seventy, my companions noted that he had been too old to acquire NSL. He was essentially "frozen" into his idiosyncratic homesign system. Why, then, I wondered, were they describing him as Deaf?

After offering him tea and snacks, my friends suggested that I video-record his life story, as I had been collecting such narratives as part of my research. Amita (my first NSL teacher and the leader of the workshop described in chapter 3) was chosen to elicit his narrative since, because of their past interactions, she had some familiarity with Madhu's homesign-ing. Though the conversation I recorded was bracketed by establishing and concluding dialogues conducted in homesign, I was surprised to see that the remainder of their talk appeared to be a seamless series of ques-tions and answers in NSL. Perhaps Madhu had been able to acquire the language after all?

Upon reviewing the videotape, however, I realized that each of his turns consisted of a repetition of the last sign in Amita's previous NSL utterance. I subsequently learned that, even though Madhu was indeed unable to produce NSL signs independently and spontaneously, he often borrowed other people's signs in socially effective ways. Madhu was not alone in this respect. I learned that many of the homesigners who had encountered Deaf social networks, but whose individual competence in NSL was com-promised by prior linguistic isolation, took advantage of the interactional scaffolding provided by others to use NSL signs they could not produce on their own.

The ideological and interactional processes that allowed some home-signers' copying of NSL signs to count as the competence needed to be considered Deaf hinged on an interaction between the karmic and the ethnolinguistic models of d/Deafness. As chapter 2 explains, the notion of the "dividual" person (Marriott 1976) contributed to the stigma of d/Deafness by suggesting that the ritual pollution of d/Deaf persons could be transferred to others through interactions with them. This perspective contributed to the social and linguistic isolation of deaf children and hence to the prevalence of homesigners in Nepal. However, this understanding of the porous nature of personhood also served to expand the inclusiveness of the ethnolinguistic model of Deafness as it was adopted in Nepal: the belief that persons could share their substance through interaction contrib-uted to local understandings of linguistic competence that hinged less on individual capabilities and more on social collaboration.

This perspective runs counter to popular and scholarly understandings of language in many Euro-American contexts, where linguistic competence is often thought of as an individual speaker's underlying knowledge of linguistic structure (e.g., Chomsky 1965). Sociolinguists and anthropologists, on the other hand, have focused on broader communicative competence (Hymes 1972), the skills required for the successful use of language in context. What constitutes such competence can vary widely within and across cultural contexts, depending on local ideologies regarding the nature of both personhood and language. The Nepali perspectives that stressed the co-construction of both language and personhood may seem unusual to some readers. However, they may help us attend to aspects of the human experience that are downplayed or obscured by models that focus on individual cognitive processes.

Indeed, attention to co-construction, the emergent collaborative creation of many aspects of human social lives, including but not limited to, language, identity, institutions, skills, emotions, and even the self (Jacoby and Ochs 1995, 171; Urban and Lee 1989), has been a tradition in a wide range of disciplines, including psychology (e.g., Vygotsky 1978; Leontyev 1981; Cole 1985; Rogoff 1990; Lave and Wenger 1991), literary theory (e.g., Bakhtin 1981; Volosinov 1973), and my own discipline, linguistic anthropology (e.g., Tedlock and Mannheim 1995; Goodwin 2004). Although this book has thus far focused on the co-constructed emergence of larger social phenomena—NSL and a Deaf jāt—this perspective also helps us understand how socially meaningful sign use *and* users are also co-constructed in interaction.

Homesigners and Late Language Acquisition

Eric Lenneberg, a linguist, first proposed a "critical period" for language acquisition in 1967. Critical periods are developmental phases during which an organism requires certain stimuli in order to develop a particular skill or capacity. For example, experiments on kittens have shown that cats require visual stimulation after birth to develop the ability to process visual signals in the brain. If such stimulus is withheld during kittenhood, the cat's ability to see does not fully develop (Wiesel and Hubel 1963). Parallel to such critical periods in biological development, humans must be exposed to sufficient language input in childhood in order for a language acquisition process to be triggered (Lenneberg 1967).

This concept has undoubtedly been controversial. Much debate on the topic focuses on "second" language acquisition by adults,[23] with scholars comparing the processes and outcomes of their learning to those of children. They have argued that the reduced fluency typically achieved by the adults supports Lenneberg's claim (e.g., Johnson and Newport 1989). Others, citing the rare cases in which adult second-language learners are able to achieve native proficiency, argue that no critical period can exist if such exceptions are possible (e.g., Hakuta, Bialystok, and Wiley 2003). Scholars who argue for a critical period have retorted that those persons who achieve nativelike competence in a language learned in adulthood do so by drawing unusually well on cognitive processes for learning that do not replicate those involved in first language acquisition (e.g., Neville 1995).

Cases in which no first languages are acquired during the proposed critical period would offer stronger evidence to either support or contradict Lenneberg's claim. Some of this research has focused on "feral" children, who have been circumstantially or purposely isolated from other people.[24] Feral children's difficulties in acquiring language after they have been recovered has been seen as supporting the critical-period hypothesis (e.g., Curtiss 1977), but the confounding abuse and possibility of prior developmental problems in many of these cases have led critics to question the validity of these studies. Children who were born deaf or became deafened before they acquired spoken language, and not thereafter exposed to an accessible language, are unfortunately more common. Research on such people indeed shows that the older a person is when first exposed to interactive language use, the less proficient the person will become. This drop-off seems to occur as early as four to six years of age (Newport, Bavelier, and Neville 2001, 483; Johnson and Newport 1989; Mayberry and Fischer 1989; Emmorey and Corina 1990; Newport 1990; Emmorey 1991; Mayberry and Eichen 1991). This work provides evidence of

---

23. I dislike the term "second language acquisition" since it implies that speakers typically have a single "first" language. In fact, growing up monolingual is not the norm; more frequently speakers natively acquire several languages.

24. Famous examples include Victor of Aveyron, a young French boy who seemed to have grown up alone in the woods, and Genie, a young girl whose abusive father kept her isolated from social contact until she was discovered in adolescence.

a critical period but shows that these maturational factors are affected by experience (Newport, Bavelier, and Neville 2001, 482).

In particular, it appears that strong stimuli can lead to learning even at an age when the critical period is beginning to close and perhaps even extend its length, whereas weaker stimuli allow for learning only at the peak of the acquisition period (Newport, Bavelier, and Neville, 494). What do scholars mean by "strong" or "weak" stimuli? Many deaf children do not have access to the strongest and most important stimulus, interactive use of language, but it is important to note that in most cases they do not exist in a communicative void. Such persons may be able to draw on the "weaker" but nonetheless accessible aspects of hearing speakers' communicative ecologies, such as gestures and facial expressions, to construct homesign systems. Though these codes are impoverished in comparison to those that have developed in a broader social and temporal milieu, they have languagelike qualities which vary in complexity (Morford 1996, 170; Goldin-Meadow 1987, 2003). Research suggests that homesigners who are exposed to a sign language after, or late in, the critical period are generally unable to achieve native proficiency. However, the degree to which they are able to learn language is affected by both age at first exposure and the structure of their particular homesign system (De Villiers et al. 1993; Morford, Singleton, and Goldin-Meadow 1995).

Age at First Exposure to Language

Deaf children who are first exposed to a sign language from school-going age through adolescence are often termed "late learners." It appears that late learners acquire vocabulary and semantic processing with nativelike fluency (Newport 1990, 484), although they often have difficulty controlling certain complex morphological processes and spatial grammatical structures common to many sign languages (Johnson and Newport 1989; Newport 1990). These constraints can, in some Deaf social networks, prevent a late learner from being considered ethnolinguistically Deaf. For example, in some parts of the globally influential Deaf culture in the United States, only native signers—that is, Deaf signers born to Deaf signing parents, who therefore acquired a sign language from birth—could claim Deaf ethnicity (LeMaster and Monaghan 2004, 147; Johnson and Erting 1989) even though less than 5 percent of d/Deaf children are born to d/Deaf parents (Mitchell and Karchmer 2004).

Though the percentage of deaf Nepalis born to deaf parents is not known, it was most likely at least as low as that cited for the United States. This is because deafness in Nepal was due more frequently to disease, iodine deficiency, or accident than to genetics (Little et al. 1993). As it was rare for hearing Nepali parents to be familiar with any sign language, those children who were profoundly and prelingually deafened were not exposed to an accessible, full-blown language in their home environment. Rather, exposure to accessible language typically occurred at school-going age at the earliest. However, there was no assurance that a given deaf child would enter school. The 1980 Report of the Sample Survey of Disabled Persons in Nepal showed that, out of an estimated 393,574 to 694,542 deaf people in Nepal, only 609 had been enrolled in school (Prasad 2003, 39). Though the number of deaf students has certainly increased since the 1980s, Nirmal Kumar Devkota (2003), a Deaf leader, estimated in 2003 that only 1 percent of deaf children had received any schooling. In addition, as mentioned earlier, because schools for deaf children in the country were few and did not exist at all before 1966, most deaf students had been enrolled in schools for hearing children, where provisions were rarely made to give such students access to the spoken and written discourse. Only those comparatively few students who entered the schools for deaf children after NSL began to emerge were exposed to an accessible language at a young age.

Consequently, during the time of my research in the 1990s and early 2000s, many members of Nepal's Deaf social networks were late learners and showed constraints similar to those described for late learners in the United States. For example, Deaf Nepalis who acquired NSL early in life produced morphologically productive combinatorial signs (e.g., combining the morphemes for TWO, YEAR, and PAST to produce a single sign: TWO-YEARS-AGO. Many late learners could not perform a single sign in this fashion but produced each morpheme independently, one after the other. However, while such constraints might endanger a late-learner's status as ethnolinguistically Deaf in some contexts in the United States, those aspects of signed grammar that are affected by late learners' prior isolation were not as relevant to dominant local ideologies about the nature of NSL, which focused on the use of standard lexical items rather than on grammatical processes. Because late learners were able to produce these lexical items, their Deaf status was unproblematic. However, many Nepali homesigners did not encounter an accessible language until adulthood (in my study, at ages ranging from nineteen to around seventy), if ever. The degree to which the homesigners in my study were able to control the lexical items of NSL when they encountered Deaf social networks in adulthood appeared to hinge in large part on the complexity of their homesign system.

Complexity of the Homesign System

My observations in Nepal suggest that a variety of social factors came into play in determining the likelihood that a given deaf person would have an opportunity to co-construct a complex homesign system that engaged the language acquisition mechanism. These systems are sometimes described as if the deaf child alone generates them. But while a deaf child's use of a homesign system is often structurally different and more languagelike than that of hearing users (Goldin-Meadow 2003), these systems require communicative interaction with willing participants. The way a family and larger community understands d/Deafness, as well as other factors such as the density of the social network in which a deaf child is embedded, can accordingly affect the quantity and quality of a deaf child's interactions and the development of a homesign system. I provide two contrasting examples from my research.

Jagajeet was born into a Newar family living in a Kirtipur. The Newars, an ethnic community considered indigenous to the region, built several important cities in the Kathmandu Valley. The old section of Kirtipur, like the other larger Newar cities (such as Patan or Bhaktapur), consisted of tightly clustered, multistoried dwellings; Jagajeet was born into this densely populated, socially complex neighborhood. He was deafened by a severe illness in infancy before he was able to acquire spoken language. Though he did not encounter a sign language until he was in his late teens, his NSL was comparable to that of late learners who acquired the language at school-going age. This may be attributable to the rich homesign system that he developed by interacting with both his immediate family and his larger community in Kirtipur.

Newar religious practices are often described as syncretic, blending elements of Tantric Hinduism and Buddhism. The stigma of d/Deafness could be less severe in some of these traditions, to Jagajeet's benefit. Residents of

Kirtipur participated in many festivals throughout the year. These required highly coordinated collaboration between households. For example, most households were members of clubs that rotated the many responsibilities involved in producing each year's Indrayani Jātrā, a street festival honoring a protective goddess. Categories of responsibility included the construction, maintenance, and physical transportation through the town of a large wooden chariot housing an image of the goddess. Jagajeet had been included in these activities throughout his life. Indeed, in addition to inviting me to join him for the 2004 jātrā, he frequently showed me large photo albums filled with images of his participation in various roles in past years' festivals. In sum, he was well integrated into this complex social network.

The homesign system he had generated by participating in these activities with his family and neighbors was more complex than many I had observed in use. When I walked through the streets of the town in his presence, I was always struck by how many neighbors greeted him and struck up conversations using homesign. For example, one evening in 2006, I walked to Kirtipur's Bāgh Bhairav temple square to meet my husband, who had been spending time there listening to the locals sing *bhajans* (devotional songs). The temple, patronized by Hindu and Buddhist practitioners, was usually a hub of activity at that time of day, with many worshippers coming to do an evening pujā. I had not planned to meet Jagajeet on this occasion but was pleased to run into him on the square, where he had been participating in a meeting of the Kirtipur Unity Committee, raising concerns about whether the temple square had been cleaned up sufficiently following a recent event.

When I greeted him, he did not switch into standard NSL, which we usually used together, but continued using the homesigns with which he had been conversing with hearing locals to inform me that my husband was nearby with the bhajan singers. I did not understand the homesign he used for "husband," which was motivated by a specifically Newar marriage practice. He realized that he had not shifted codes and laughingly began to give me a brief lesson (with participation from the hearing Newars present) about differences between the homesigns used in his neighborhood and NSL. In sum, one may presume that the greater complexity and wider social distribution of this homesign system had helped him retain the capacity to learn NSL later in life.

By contrast, Hema, who was also deafened before acquiring spoken language, was very socially isolated. She lived in a small village in Mustang, a sparsely populated, arid region near Tibet. Growing up, she spent most of her days in the hills with the family's livestock—work that she could do well despite being deaf but which kept her alone much of the time. Eventually she was married to a deaf man from another settlement, whose youth had been spent in a similar manner and who continued to do this work as an adult. Because her mother-in-law was deceased, often the only family members at home were Hema and her father-in-law, Dawa. During an afternoon I spent visiting Hema, I had been hoping to observe any homesigns the two might have constructed, but, despite the fact that only the two of them were at home, they never communicated directly with one another but only with me.

Finally, I attempted to initiate such an interaction by asking Dawa to ask Hema a particular question. He looked uncomfortable and did not comply. My companion that day, a hearing American with longer experience in that region, nudged me and whispered that in this particular cultural setting, a father-in-law and his daughter-in-law were not supposed to address one another directly. Ideally, the mother-in-law would mediate their communication. In her absence, unnecessary direct conversation was still avoided whenever possible. Thus, as in childhood, in adulthood Hema spent most of her time alone or in uncommunicative company. Readers will not be surprised to learn that her homesign system, elements of which we were eventually able to record, appeared to be quite rudimentary.

Unfortunately, during the period of my research it was common for many Nepali homesigners to grow up in environments more similar to Hema's than Jagajeet's. Due to the stigma of d/Deafness, many did not have a rich network of willing partners in creating homesign systems. If homesigners encountered Deaf social life and NSL in adulthood, those who had experienced extreme linguistic and social isolation of long duration were often constrained in their ability to independently produce even the lexical items of NSL. This inability did not resolve itself with exposure over time. Several homesigners in my study appeared to be "frozen" into their idiosyncratic gestural system despite daily interaction in the associations of Deaf people for more than ten years. For example, my good friend Radha, a homesigner who encountered Deaf social life and NSL in middle age, was a daily fixture in the KAD. However, over the now eighteen years in which I have known her, and despite her exposure to NSL at the KAD, her linguistic repertoire has not significantly expanded.

Copying and Mirroring in Nepal's Associations of Deaf People

Studies of ethnolinguistic perspectives on Deafness rarely discuss home-signers, focusing instead on families in which d/Deafness is hereditary, such that sign language and cultural identity are acquired from birth at home. Research that does discuss the role of homesigners often points to their exclusion from Deafness as a social category in this model. For example, one study (Senghas 2003, 270) reports that signers in Nicaragua's Deaf social networks, who had adopted an ethnolinguistic model of Deafness, referred to homesigners unable acquire sign language as NO-SABE ("know-nothing") (ibid.), a term similar to the Nepali word *lāṭo*. However, in the remainder of this chapter I show that how an ethnolinguistic model of Deafness affects the status of homesigners depends on local ideologies regarding competence and personhood.

Members of Nepal's associations of Deaf people regularly sent young Deaf men and women into rural areas to recruit nonhearing persons into Deaf social life. Though an important goal of these efforts was to expose deaf children to NSL at an early age, adults were also included in these outreach efforts. As a result, eighteen of the roughly sixty persons I worked with in Nepal's associations of Deaf people were homesigners with impaired abilities to acquire NSL. Even though around ten of these persons had difficulty with or were unable to produce the standard NSL signs independently and spontaneously, they frequently copied or mirrored their interlocutor's signs. When I say "mirroring," I mean that some homesigners replicated the signs in reverse, like a reflection in a mirror.[25] Copying is

---

25. Sign language users who are right-handed will typically use their right hand as the "dominant" hand when signing. That means that the right hand will be the hand used in performing signs that only require one hand, and that in two-handed signs, the right hand will be the more active hand. Left-handed signers will typically reverse this pattern. While my research did not focus on the role of "handed-ness" in homesign systems, a review of my video data showed home-signers in my study demonstrating right handedness when using their homesign systems but reversing this dominance when mirroring.

a more complex practice than mirroring, as it involves taking into account the different spatial orientation of each party. (Readers who have ever participated in a dance or an aerobics class in which the instructor alternates between facing the front of the room and facing the class members will likely have experienced the comparative difficulty of copying rather than mirroring movements when face to face with an instructor.) Although my research on this phenomenon is still in progress, the length and degree of linguistic isolation appeared to be predictive of whether a homesigner would copy or mirror. Specifically, the more extreme the isolation, the more likely it was that a person would mirror rather than copy.

Copying or mirroring had the greatest impact on a homesigner's potential status as Deaf when it occurred in the context of two important speech events at the associations of Deaf persons: formal NSL classes run by these associations and the life story narratives members told each other about the events that had led them to join these organizations. The following excerpts were recorded between October 2004 and May 2005 at the NDFN in Kathmandu and in an NSL classroom in Pharping.

Nepali Sign Language Classes

As discussed in chapter 3, in addition to having created the dictionaries codifying the lexical items that constituted NSL in local ideologies, the associations of Deaf people held classes to disseminate and reinforce the standard signs. Students in these classes included recruits who were deafened later in life and were acquiring NSL as a second language, fluent signers who wished to better align their way of signing with the standard practice, hearing students who planned to become interpreters or teachers or had d/Deaf family members, and also homesigners who had encountered Deaf social networks when they were too old to enter the schools for d/Deaf children.

A class held in 2004 in Pharping is a good example of the structure of these classes during my research. Four d/Deaf adults (two of whom were prelingually deafened homesigners who had not encountered an accessible language until early adulthood) and two young hearing participants were present at this lesson. All of the participants lived with their families in or around Pharping. As explained in chapter 3, the instructor, Birendra, was a member of one of the first cohorts of Deaf students to be exposed to the emerging NSL at a young age and a high-ranking leader at the KAD.

When the class began, Birendra turned to a list of verbs he had written in Nepali on the blackboard and, pointing to each, modeled its NSL translation (the written Nepali forms were for the benefit of the hearing participants and for the Deaf signers who had received schooling; the homesigners present were not literate). His introduction of these signs did not include any instruction on how they would be used in context, though in practice Deaf signers modified verbs to reflect, for example, person, aspect, or tense. This pedagogical focus, which was in accordance with the previously described ideological focus on lexical items, was consistent with all other NSL classes I had observed and participated in since 1997. Students learned grammatical aspects of NSL not through formal instruction but through social interaction.

After their teacher's presentation of the signs to the class, the students were individually asked to perform each sign from memory. Jeevan, who was deafened later in childhood, by which time he had acquired a good deal of spoken Nepali, went first. He came to the front of the classroom and began repeating the signs that Birendra had modeled. However, he performed a nonstandard version of TO-UNDERSTAND. At this, Birendra stopped Jeevan and demonstrated the standard form again, which Jeevan repeated. Jeevan then went on to recite the rest of the signs correctly (see transcript 3). Essentially, Jeevan was expected to produce the signs without prompting, and Birendra supplied the sign form only if Jeevan hesitated too long or produced it incorrectly. The two hearing students performed the task in the same fashion.

Transcript 3

Jeevan:
1. to know

Jeevan:
1. TO-KNOW

Jeevan:
2. to understand (nonstandard form)

Jeevan:
2. TO-UNDERSTAND (nonstandard form)

Birendra:
3. to understand (standard form)

Birendra:
3. TO-UNDERSTAND (standard form)

Jeevan:
4. to understand (standard form)

Jeevan:
4. TO-UNDERSTAND (standard form)

The procedure shifted when the homesigners were called to the board, as illustrated by the turn taken by Usha, a homesigner first exposed to language in her early twenties. Rather than expecting Usha to produce the forms independently, Birendra required only that she produce each sign correctly by directly copying as he modeled each one (see transcript 4). Of course, the other students had themselves been copying the model Birendra had provided at the beginning of the class, while Birendra himself was copying the forms from the NSL dictionary. However, most of the participants were expected to internalize and independently reproduce the forms in a way that the homesigners, such as Usha, were not. The other homesigner in attendance that day likewise copied as Birendra proceeded through the recitation. This was not because the homesigners were new to the class. Rather, this arrangement had been reached only when it became clear that they were unlikely to learn to produce the signs independently.

Transcript 4

Birendra:
1. To do

Birendra:
1. TO-DO

Usha:
2. To do

Usha:
2. TO-DO

Birendra:
3. To stay

Birendra:
3. TO-STAY

Usha:
4. To stay

Usha:
4. TO-STAY

This method of incorporating homesigners into the language lessons was common throughout the five regional associations for Deaf people whose NSL classes I observed. In addition, while most of the students discontinued their participation in the classes after having mastered the standard signs, many homesigners continued to attend the NSL classes, never acquiring the ability to produce the standard forms independently but performing them in concert with their teachers several times a week. Their continued participation in these lessons suggests that the classes served not only to teach the standard forms of NSL to those who could learn them but also to provide a forum in which such homesigners who could not learn these standardized forms could publicly perform them with the teachers' support.

Emplacement Stories

Because most d/Deaf children are born to hearing parents, Deaf cultures have been characterized as "convert cultures," which one must typically join rather than be born into (Bechter 2008). Those who enter Deaf social networks in Nepal often talked about the path that had brought them there and through that narrative firmly located themselves within a milieu defined by an ethnolinguistic model of deafness. Most of the life stories I recorded detailed their experience of having first suffered the shame of being defined as ritually polluted and their joy at having discovered the alternative ethnolinguistic framework. Following Kirin Narayan (2002, 425), I call such narratives "emplacement" stories, as their telling is part of an emplacement process, both a strategy of coming to belong somewhere and a discursive "orientation of the self within multiple frameworks of meaning."

Bahirā Āwāj (*Voice of Deaf*), a publication of the NADH (Now NDFN) which collected members' poems, remembrances, and notices, included many such stories. A submission from Dipawali (Dipa) Sharmacharya is a particularly evocative example of the genre. It begins with a remembrance from Dipa's early childhood, before she was deafened, when she first heard the sounds of a motor vehicle. This occurred in the context of her family's relocation by bus from the hills to a village in the Terai: "When I heard the 'beep beep' sound from far away, I asked my mother what is that sound, where is it coming from? Because in my village I had not heard such a sound, only the jackal and tigers" (2000, 9). When the bus arrived, Dipa was surprised by its size: "[T]here were too many people crowded inside it, people were popping their heads out. I started thinking, the houses and mountains are long but the bus is long like a house that is moving" (ibid., 9).

What she describes as a "storm in her life" occurred after the move, when, at age eight or nine, she contracted typhoid. As the "only daughter in the family" she received proper care and survived but lost her hearing. Because she was deafened after acquiring spoken Nepali, and because of her intelligence, she continued to succeed in school. However, "I was an odd man out in the society where everyone else could hear . . . I was forced to accept all the humiliation, discrimination, and isolation." Finally, through some family connections, she learned "that there [were] many deaf students in Kathmandu" and went there to study NSL "despite hesitation and fear" that, "coming from a remote village," she might not "adapt well to city life." However, she adapted so well to signing and the Deaf social world that she became "lost in it," ultimately becoming an NSL teacher herself (ibid., 10).

Some years later Dipa was given an opportunity, through alliances between transnational associations of Deaf people, to visit Sweden, then a major source of funding for Nepali institutions for Deaf persons. Her story includes an experience parallel to her childhood encounter with the bus, when she discusses her first ride in an airplane, with reference to the visual and tactile elements of the journey. She then recounts the deep affective ties she formed with Deaf signers in Sweden, likening them to her kin (ibid., 11). Ultimately, then, Dipa's story emplaces her not only in Deaf social life in Nepal but also in transnational Deaf networks.

Homesigners tell these stories as well, often using their homesign systems. However, because the thrust of these stories was generally to emplace the teller in a Deaf social life and identity, and because such status was increasingly defined by the use of NSL, these stories were most successfully told using the standard NSL signs. To illustrate the manner in which some homesigners who were unable to produce such signs independently collaborated with fluent signers to tell their emplacement stories using NSL, I return to the conversation between Amita and Madhu with which this chapter opened. Amita, who was chosen to interview Madhu because she had some familiarity with his homesign system, was a respected NSL teacher seen as highly competent in the language. Because Amita was not deafened until around eight years of age, she had already acquired spoken Nepali, and her signing was often influenced by spoken Nepali word order. Although in the United States her signing might therefore be considered nonnative, potentially problematizing Amita's status as ethnolinguistically Deaf, her command of the standard lexical items meant that her Deaf status was not questioned in Nepal.

Before their collaborative emplacement story began, Amita told me what she already knew about Madhu's background. She said that he lived at the Pashupatinath temple, the most important Hindu temple complex in Nepal. To make a living, he set out from the temple grounds each day carrying a leaf with mud from the riverbed on it. He would then offer to put *ṭikā* on the heads of passersby—in other words, to smear a bit of the mud on their forehead with the third finger of his right hand. This bestowed blessings on the recipients, who were then expected to offer him a small financial reward (the act of giving the money also allows the giver to accrue merit and thus is beneficial to both parties).

The association of a d/Deaf person with this Hindu religious activity might seem at odds with the karmic conception of d/Deafness described in this book. However, the Pashupatinath temple complex was a site at which *sādhus,* or ascetics, played with and subverted rules about pollution. The site was also home to charity organizations serving many who might be considered polluted in other contexts. These factors may have affected Madhu's ability to make a living in this way. About two years prior to this meeting, in the course of his perambulations around the city, he had encountered Nanu, a young Deaf woman who encouraged him to include the associations of Deaf people on his route. The associations had since become daily stops, where he put ṭikā on all those present, received some money, and then stopped to socialize.

Amita then confirmed Madhu's given name by inspecting the identification card he wore around his neck (such cards were frequently worn by those d/Deaf people in Nepal who did not read or write). She next estimated his age by extrapolating from his recollection, conveyed through homesign, that he was six years old when the last major earthquake struck Kathmandu, in 1934 (that is, prior to the devastating 2015 earthquake). Because this conversation occurred in 2004, Amita estimated that he was seventy-six years old. She then inquired about his relatives, most of whom, he reported, were now deceased. Transcript 5 opens as she began to inquire about his relationship with a younger brother he had mentioned. She asked about their medium of communication and, on being told that they no longer met or talked, shifted the time frame to their mutual childhoods in order to learn how they communicated then (Madhu had been born deaf). She concluded that the brothers had employed "natural signs," or homesigns.

Transcript 5 highlights the way in which Madhu borrowed Amita's signs. While it is possible to positively identify mirroring (as opposed to copying) only in a sign that involves a difference in the shape, orientation, or movement of the hand on one side of the signing space (a perfectly symmetrical sign looks the same regardless of whether it is copied or mirrored), Madhu mirrored rather than copied all of the asymmetrical signs. In both the translation (in the left-hand column) and the English gloss (in the right-hand column), the underlined sections indicate points at which Madhu has borrowed Amita's signs; sections in italics indicate that the sign is a mirror image of her form.

Transcript 5:

Amita:
1. You, hey, you and your younger brother, do you talk together?

Amita:
1. YOU, HEY, YOU YOUNGER-BROTHER. YOU HE YOU-AND-HE-TALK WHAT?

Madhu:
2. _No._

Madhu:
2. _WHAT_ (neg).

Amita:
3. Do you sign?

Amita:
3. YOU-SIGN?

Madhu:
4. No, <u>we don't sign.</u>

Madhu:
4. <u>SIGN</u> NO.

Amita:
5. You and your brother, you don't meet?

Amita:
5. YOUNGER-BROTHER YOU NOT-MEET NOT?

Madhu:
6. _No, we don't meet._

Madhu:
6. _NOT-MEET NOT_

Amita:
7. Before, when you were both young, you, when you were both young . . .

Amita:
7. PAST MUTUAL-CHILDHOODS YOU, MUTUAL CHILDHOODS.

Madhu:
8. _When we both were young,_ yes.

Madhu:
8. _MUTUAL-CHILDHOODS_ YES.

Amita:
9. Your younger brother was hearing and you were not—what (did you do)?

Amita:
9. BROTHER HE HEARING YOU NOT YOU WHAT (did you do)?

Madhu:
10. _What_ (could we do)?

Madhu:
10. _WHAT_ (could we do)?

Amita:
11. You sort of signed?

Amita:
11. YOU SORT-OF-SIGNED?

Madhu:
12. <u>Sort of signed.</u>

Madhu:
12. SORT-OF-SIGNED.

Amita:
13. (to onlooker) Natural sign.

Amita:
13. (to onlooker) NATURAL SIGN.

(Madhu interjects to explain in homesign that he had been cheated out of his inheritance.)

Amita:

14. They did *not* give you your portion.

Amita:

14. YOU-NOT PORTION NOT-GIVE-YOU *NOT*.

Madhu:

15. <u>No.</u>

Madhu:

15. <u>NOT.</u>

The members of the associations of Deaf people and my subsequent observations confirmed that Madhu did not independently produce standard NSL signs, except for those that overlapped with his homesign system, such as the movements of the head or hand indicating "yes" or "no" (which were common in hearing persons' communicative repertoires as well). Despite this, he used standard NSL signs in each of the utterances in transcript 5. Other than the aforementioned signs that overlapped with his homesigns, the standard forms were mirrored appropriations of signs in Amita's immediately prior utterances. However, in line 15, Amita reversed the orientation of her sign; consequently, Madhu's mirrored response took on the correct standard form.[26] The iconicity thus produced between his signing and standard NSL forms reflected—and in so doing produced— Madhu as a competent user of NSL.

Though the degree to which Madhu understood the NSL signs he produced cannot be stated with certainty, his role in copying and mirroring was active rather than passive. He had to be able to time his contributions to the ongoing conversation effectively. Furthermore, in order for his mirrored signs to function as negative or affirmative answers to Amita's questions, Madhu had to deploy prosodic features appropriately by, in his responses, omitting the raised brows that marked Amita's utterances as questions.

However, this sort of contextually appropriate copying or mirroring did not rely on the abilities of homesigners alone but inherently required the cooperation of their partners. Amita had to phrase her questions in such a way that they could be successfully responded to by repeating their last sign. Because Madhu mirrored rather than copied asymmetrical signs, even this did not consistently allow him to produce formally correct NSL signs until, consciously or unconsciously, Amita reversed the orientation of her sign so that his mirrored appropriation was formally correct. Some homesigners were more likely than others to find cooperative partners for

---

26. In declaring this form "correct" I am assuming right-handedness, which Madhu displayed.

such interactions, their prospects mediated by other aspects of their multi-jāt personhoods, such as age, class, or caste. Madhu attracted this support because of his age, in a Nepali cultural context in which it was important to honor elders and a Deaf cultural context in which elderly people were rare and exciting.

I witnessed and recorded other interactions in which fluent signers, unwilling to share signs, positioned their bodies so that homesigners with less social status were unable to copy them. For example, several weeks after I recorded Madhu's life story, Shiva, another homesigner, visited the association. He appeared to be in his thirties. I asked whether I could record his life story as well. A young Deaf signer named Deepak, who had some familiarity with Shiva's homesigns, was recruited to facilitate the narration. However, rather than initiate a coordinated interaction through which Shiva could tell his emplacement story through standard signs, Deepak stepped between Shiva and my camera and began to tell the story himself, at one point recruiting Shiva's NSL teacher, Pitambur, to comment. In several places, when Shiva himself attempted to contribute to the telling, Deepak signed over him and once even physically swatted at his hands to interrupt his efforts. Thus, Shiva was unable to tell a story that successfully emplaced him as Deaf. Transcript 6 follows the same conventions as in transcript 5.

Transcript 6

Deepak:
1. In the past, when he was growing up, he wasn't in school.

2. I (Deepak) went to school growing up, it helped me. I worked from then on and met people, talked with them, learned language, and became independent.

3. He (Shiva) was the same as a beggar growing up.

4. In his village there was a project where he studied sign language, and then he moved here.

Deepak:
1. HE PAST HE GROWING-UP HE WASN'T-IN-SCHOOL.

2. I SCHOOL GROWING-UP HELPED ME THEN WORKED FROM-THEN MET-PEOPLE TALKED-TO-OTHERS LANGUAGE BECAME-INDEPENDENT.

3. HE GROWING-UP SAME BEGGAR SAME.

4. VILLAGE THERE VILLAGE PROJECT SIGN STUDY FINISH MOVE-HERE.

After thus beginning to tell Shiva's story (and mentioning his own background as a point of comparison), Deepak called on Pitambur, who had been Shiva's NSL instructor in the village project. Pitambur commented that, although Shiva seemed to understand much of what was signed to him, he was ultimately too old to learn NSL. (It was only in the previous year that Shiva had been introduced to NSL.) While Pitambur signed, Shiva tried to interject but was ignored.

Transcript 6 (Continued):

Pitambur:
5. He doesn't have a job. He searches for work but hasn't found any.

Pitambur:
5. HE WORK DOESN'T-HAVE SEARCHES HE WORK SEARCHES DOESN'T-HAVE.

Shiva:
6. (I) <u>search.</u>

Shiva:
6. <u>SEARCH</u>

Deepak then moved his body to block Shiva's visual access to both Pitambur and the camera.

Deepak:
7. Hey—he has his own house—hey—house!

Deepak:
7. HEY HOUSE HIS-OWN HEY HOUSE!

Shiva again attempted to sign something, but Deepak physically swatted his hands down. Then, addressing me, he explained that he considered it fruitless to allow Shiva to tell me his own story in homesign.

Transcript 6 (Continued):

Deepak:
8. You won't understand each other.

Deepak:
8. YOU-WON'T UNDERSTAND-EACH-OTHER.

As line 6 shows, Shiva attempted to participate in the conversation by borrowing Pitambur's previous sign, SEARCH. With a willing partner, this interaction might have been as socially effective as Madhu and Amita's. However, Deepak was not a willing partner, frequently blocking Shiva's attempts to borrow signs and finally physically preventing him from signing. It may not surprise readers to learn that Deepak did not refer to Shiva as Deaf but as lāṭo, as this sort of interaction not only indexed an assessment of him as such but also worked to produce his membership in that category.[27] Madhu's inclusion and Shiva's exclusion from a Deaf category hinged as much on the differences in social support they could attract as on their individual competencies.

Sharing Substance, Sharing Competence

When homesigners copy or mirror signs, their individual intentionality and the degree to which their signing reflects an understanding of the linguistic forms can be unclear or inaccessible. This fact is exacerbated by the inherently collaborative nature of the interactions.. Within some cultural contexts, including much of Euro-America, this would cause many people to deny or seriously doubt the validity of framing Usha's or Madhu's copying as evidence that they are Deaf users of NSL. Indeed, some readers may find Deepak's assessment of Shiva's lack of competence more reasoned and appropriate than the attribution of competence to Usha or Madhu. However, this perspective is not purely objective but is itself mediated by language ideologies; in particular, *personalism,* a dominant ideology in many Euro-American contexts, according to which it is assumed that "the most important part of linguistic meaning comes from the beliefs and intentions of the speaker" (Hill 2008, 88–89).

This perspective is by no means universal. In some cultural contexts, attempts to uncover the intentions of other speakers are strongly discouraged or the right or obligation to do so is distributed only to certain parties in an interaction (Ochs and Schieffelin 1984). In other contexts the effects of utterances, including the social relationships they create or reinforce, are given ideological precedence (Rosaldo 1982; Duranti 1994). In yet other cases, the production of linguistic meaning independently of the intention of the speaker is idealized (Du Bois 1993). As the previous chapters have illustrated, in Nepal the individual was not as privileged a category as in many Euro-American contexts. Persons were not seen as bounded and discrete units but as permeable and transformable through interactions with others. Consequently, the blurred lines of authorship and intentionality that occurred in cases of collaborative copying and mirroring did not undermine the attribution of competence to homesigners but instead

---

27. Similarly, Green (2014, 47) thoughtfully argues that the broader campaign carried out by the associations of Deaf people against use of the term lāṭo is "not only a protest about being perceived as lāṭo but also being made lāṭo."

supported it; by sharing their signs, competent signers were also able to share their competence.

As mentioned at the beginning of this chapter, much research in a variety of disciplines explores the usefulness of approaching both language and personhood as co-constructed and emergent from social interaction. Such scholars' work often recalls Marriott's (1976) description of the "dividual" person. For example, psychologists have argued that participants' beliefs, practices, and identities can be so mutually influential that they can each at least partially constitute the other (Jacoby and Ochs 1995, 173; Leontyev 1981) and that joint participation in social events often entails the appropriation of others' skills (Rogoff 1990). Language use is one such skill: However individual or private our use of language might seem, all language use emerges from our past (and projected future) interactions with others (Bakhtin 1981; Jacoby and Ochs 1995). While such co-constructedness may in fact be universal, the ways in which these processes reflect and produce social identities and roles of participants vary according to the situation. Beliefs about the nature of personhood and language, whether they are grounded in "personalism," a notion of the "dividual" person, or other ideologies, affect the ways in which people enact and interpret these processes of co-construction. Such beliefs—and their consequences—are not static but likewise change in relation to social contexts and historical periods.

This point was highlighted for me on a visit to Nepal in 2015. While in 1997 Shrihari had frankly asserted that Nepal had no old Deaf people, from 2008 on, the KAD, with funding from the British organization Deafway, had begun hosting a program called the Old Deaf Project (ODP). Under the auspices of this program, elder d/Deaf Nepalis gathered several times a week at the association where members served them snacks and tea and organized activities such as art projects. The most enriching aspect of the ODP, association members noted, was that it provided the elderly d/Deaf people an opportunity to engage in Deaf sociality, both with each other and with younger signers. This was especially important because it was reported that their hearing family members rarely engaged with them socially or communicatively.

The first time I visited the ODP I was especially hoping to reunite with Madhu, as after our first meeting (with which I opened the chapter) he and I had enjoyed regularly drinking tea together at the association. I was not disappointed. He was there, wearing a warm wooly hat to ward off the January chill. His ODP cohort included other homesigners I had long known, such as Radha, who had never ceased to participate cheerfully in association events. She had not been considered elderly by association members during earlier phases of my research but had aged into the category over the many years I had known her. A few other members had once been active participants at the associations of Deaf persons but had disappeared for some years, finally rejoining through this group. Other participants were newly recruited to the association, located by members who canvassed the surrounding neighborhoods for elderly nonhearing Nepalis that might benefit from the nutritional and social support offered by the program.

The linguistic repertoires of ODP members varied widely: Some had been deafened in adulthood and audibly voiced spoken Nepali or Newar Bhāṣā (Newar language), supplemented with NSL signs they had been taught at the association. For example, one afternoon as I was chatting with Tashi (a younger signer I had known for many years), Hisila, a member of the ODP, interjected in a mixture of voiced Newar Bhāṣā and NSL signs that Tashi had many SPOUSES. Being new to NSL, she had signed SPOUSES rather than FRIENDS, though her voicing, lip movements, and status as a fledgling signer had made it easy to recover her intended meaning. Tashi laughed and corrected her, commenting to me that, although she was old, she was a new signer. Other ODP members, deafened at birth or in childhood but newly recruited to signing networks, communicated using their idiosyncratic homesign systems, many of which overlapped where they had incorporated cospeech gestures in wide use in Nepal (e.g., a shaking hand for negation; a flip of the wrist to indicate a question). As I joined them for tea and cookies, I watched the elders copy or mirror not only the younger fluent signers attending to them but also one another, incorporating all of the participants into a successful social interaction that both reflected and maintained the fact that, by then, there certainly were old Deaf people in Nepal.

To conclude, so far this book has focused on how karmic and ethnolinguistic models of deafness interacted in producing a Deaf jāt, while also attending to the ideologically mediated linguistic processes through which signers managed both the inclusions and potential exclusions of nonhearing Nepalis this process entailed. But what about hearing Nepalis who engaged with Deaf signers, who were becoming increasingly prominent in public places in Kathmandu? Through what ideological models did hearing Nepalis interpret these engagements and what were the effects of these interactions? This issue is explored in the next chapter.

"Action Speaks": Producing Bikāsi Hearing People in the Bakery Café

5

In 2008, the Bakery Café, a popular and relatively expensive restaurant chain in Nepal, aired a television advertisement promoting its venues. The commercial featured a waiter performing a series of NSL signs for fast-food items such as burgers, *momos* (dumplings), pizza, and coffee, with written English translations appearing on screen. The piece concluded with the written words "Action Speaks," followed by the Bakery Café logo. In addition to advertising menu items, this commercial (and similar ones the chain subsequently aired) also publicized the fact that several of the Bakery Café outlets featured Deaf waitstaff. Further, the commercial implied that, rather than expect the Deaf waitstaff to speak or read lips, patrons might use the featured NSL signs to place their orders.

Why would a Nepali restaurant televise such an ad? The previous chapters have described a long-standing association between d/Deafness and ritual pollution in Nepal. Given that food was an especially effective medium for transmitting said pollution, hiring Deaf waiters to serve in a restaurant chain—and explicitly advertising their presence—might seem highly inadvisable. As previous chapters have shown, however, associations of Deaf persons had been working to contest the association between Deafness and ritual pollution. Furthermore, while karma and an attendant belief in ritual pollution remained significant idioms for structuring social relations at the time the commercial was shown, *bikās* (development), class, and modernity had increasingly come to coexist and/or compete with karma as important social frameworks. One illustration of the cultural salience of these concepts in Nepal—since it opened its borders to international trade and aid in the post-Rana period—was the fact that Bikās had become a common given name, a means of signaling hope that a child so named would display this quality (Liechty 2003). (Likewise, the NSL sign BIKĀS, which also meant "development," was also sometimes used as a group-internal name sign by Deaf Nepalis, applied to those whose given Nepali name was Bikās and/or those deemed especially devoted to pursuing development initiatives.)

However, even as development and modernity became highly valued social qualities, Nepalis were exposed to transnational discourses that positioned them as the opposite of modern (Pigg 1996, 163). These frameworks functioned, in part, to attract aid: Nepal received an estimated US$3.7 billion between 1951 and 1997 (Joshi 1997). Though this money was routed through the urban capital, Kathmandu (and much of it stayed there, having been filtered through many bureaucratic bodies and non-governmental organizations), the money was typically intended for rural areas, as their "undeveloped" qualities attracted the aid. Other major components of Nepal's economy included tourism and remittances from abroad. These industries were also deeply invested in an image of Nepal as traditional and premodern (Pigg 1996; Liechty 2003).[28]

Consequently, an important social project for many Nepalis became the transformation of Nepali modernity from an oxymoron to a reality (Liechty 2003, 7). Kathmandu's Bakery Café restaurants were one context in which this project was enacted, providing an environment in which customers were transformed from "aid receivers" to "aid givers" through their interaction with Deaf servers. The fact that Deaf waiters would "traditionally" be understood as transmitting pollution did not undermine this effect; rather, it was precisely the reason that the practice of accepting food from Deaf servers functioned to generate and display customers' modern and bikāsi ("developed") personas. Thus, this practice simultaneously combated and benefited from the stigma of deafness during this period.

Deafness, Development, and Employment

As already mentioned, many transnational organizations, both governmental and nongovernmental, have engaged with d/Deaf Nepalis. These

---

28. However, during my research in the 2000s, both the flow of aid and the ideological goals of the state were increasingly affected by the Maoist war, which ended in 2006 and led to an ongoing reconfiguration of the government (discussed in the final chapter).

groups have often echoed the development discourse described earlier. That is, they typically described d/Deaf Nepalis' low social position, health problems, and lack of educational and economic opportunities as caused by Nepal's lack of development and modernity. They argued that it was this "backwardness" that led to the stigmatization of d/Deaf people rather than an inherent quality on the part of d/Deaf persons (as a karma framework would suggest). Many of these organizations focused explicitly on providing employment opportunities for d/Deaf Nepalis, ideally freeing them from dependence on birth social networks, which adhered to a "backward" view of d/Deafness.

Indeed, employment in Nepal was often either inherited (by jāt) or obtained via family connections. As a consequence, the expelling of d/Deaf Nepalis from their birth castes (either simply as a result of their deafness or as a result of marrying a Deaf partner from an inappropriate birth jāt) could have serious material, as well as social, consequences.[29] Those d/Deaf Nepalis who were rejected by their families or viewed as incapable of participating meaningfully in the family's work often participated in skill-training programs provided by organizations serving d/Deaf people. For example, during my time at the Lumbini Association of the Deaf, my friend Shrihari spent several hours each afternoon on the balcony of the building learning to make candles. The Pokhara Association of the Deaf dedicated a room in its building to training youth in making handicrafts from bamboo. But tailoring was by far the most frequent type of skill training, offered by many schools and associations of Deaf persons, as well as international organizations.

In 2004 and 2005 I frequently visited Kathmandu's Swedish Sewing Project, where, as explained earlier, d/Deaf women from primarily rural areas lived in an on-site dormitory, studied NSL and Nepali, and learned to sew. Having come to know the students through a series of interviews

---

29. Of course, this did not always occur; many Deaf Nepalis in my study were employed in their family's line of work. A few examples include Gaurav, who worked at his family's printing shop; Pema, who was trained by her family to paint *thangkas,* colorful depictions of scenes from the life of the Buddha, or *maṇḍalas* (circular patterns representing the universe); or Dawa, who served as a porter when his Sherpa family led tourists on treks.

and many sessions spent observing and recording their language and sewing classes, I was invited to a party for the graduating cohort. It was the end of the winter monsoon season in Kathmandu, bone-chilling cold and damp inside the concrete school building but pleasant that afternoon on the sunny rooftop, where the celebration was held.[30] Younger students danced to fete the graduates, visiting representative from the local associations of Deaf people gave laudatory speeches, and snacks were served to all. The happiness of the affair was mitigated by the fact that, like Maya in chapter 3, many of the girls did not look forward to returning to their home villages, where their new NSL skills would be difficult to use. Though the goal of the program was to prepare the students to find work in existing tailor shops in their family's villages, the head of the program complained to me that most of the graduates sought to remain in Kathmandu or to go to another urban center where they could be around other Deaf signers. The problem with this aim, the tailoring instructors felt, was that the tailor shops in a given city might not be willing or able to absorb so many d/Deaf employees; better that they be dispersed.

In countering this concern, several of the signers cited the success of Laxmi Thakali's Chup Chap (Silent) Tailor Shop in Pokhara during the 1990s. Originally from the Mustang region, Laxmi was one of the first graduates of the earliest schools for d/Deaf students in Nepal. Upon graduating, he married a fellow Deaf student, a Hindu woman from the Terai region. This dramatically cross-jāt union led to their both being cut off financially and socially from their families. Having received training in tailoring as part of his schooling, Laxmi opened up shop for himself, assisted by his wife, charging less than local hearing tailors in order to attract customers. As his business grew, he began to hire additional Deaf staff who were recruited from the local schools for d/Deaf students. The "all-deaf" shop became a notable feature in Pokhara, which was a popular tourist destination, the largest urban gateway to several popular trekking routes.[31]

---

30. Monsoon seasons do not involve rain all day long but rather significant bursts of rain almost every day.

31. Trekking, a popular tourist activity taking advantage of Nepal's spectacular terrain, is similar to hiking but differs in that treks are typically of longer duration (days or weeks). Trekkers usually overnight in Nepali homes or lodges (rather than

Laxmi later relocated to work as a general assistant for the Lumbini Association of the Deaf,[32] though the Chup Chap shop continued for some time to thrive in Pokhara with a Deaf staff. Thus, while the directors of the Swedish Sewing Project were concerned about the importance of dispersing Deaf tailors, the Chup Chap shop provided an alternative model of a business that explicitly concentrated and advertised a d/Deaf presence.

However, tailoring was usually associated with low-caste status in Nepal. As a result, instruction in tailoring potentially reinforced the widespread indexical associations between d/Deafness and ritual pollution. When I asked Sanjay, a prominent member of the Kathmandu Association of the Deaf, whether this sort of occupational training might work against the association's efforts to forge indexical connections between standard NSL, a Deaf jāt, and high-caste markers of ritual purity, he began by signing that, although caste had "long ago" been divisive, it was no longer important in Nepal. He said that if low-caste people were able to study and obtain a degree, they abandoned their traditional occupations. As such, he claimed, occupation and jāt no longer mapped cleanly onto one another. I then asked whether it would be strange for a Deaf Bāhun (i.e., someone born into a very high caste) to enter a d/Deaf occupational program that teaches tailoring. He replied, signing, "If I were a Deaf signing Bāhun, I'd sew. If I wanted work and food and was hungry—what-do-do? Sewing. I'd go study and get work sewing. I—There is! In Gorkha there is one Deaf Bāhun tailor who sews, sells, and profits financially! He is Deaf. I was surprised!"

The amazed glee with which Sanjay reported this fact belied his earlier bland assertions that caste no longer mattered in occupational choices. In

---

in tents) and typically hire Nepali porters to carry their gear (rather than carrying their own supplies in backpacks).

32. I became close with Laxmi and his wife during my first trip to Nepal in 1997. The couple took me out for an afternoon snack most days, introducing me to a surprisingly tasty spaghetti substitute: ketchup poured over instant chow mein noodles. They encouraged me to speak in English with their hearing son (who was fluent in both Nepali and NSL and was learning English at school). But much of the time we chatted on the porch of the association of Deaf people, where Laxmi, when not running errands for the association, continued to sew for fun and profit.

fact, when announcing the existence of the Deaf Bāhun tailor, he repeated himself several times and made eye contact with all the other Deaf signers in the association room that day, grinning as they, too, expressed surprise. In this respect, Sanjay's narrative revealed competing perspectives: the official voices of the association of Deaf people and of the development projects, which, in promoting tailoring as an occupational choice, had asserted that traditional meanings no longer needed to attach to caste identity or previously jāt-based occupations, and a voice that contradicted that claim, as he recounted as noteworthy a rare experience that actually fit that ideal. For in fact, it was largely true that Deaf individuals who had found success as a result of tailor training were not from upper-caste families (unless they had been rejected by said families and lost caste status) but were typically lower-caste Hindus or members of ādivāsi janajāti (indigenous nationalities).

The Bakery Café

Another highly visible employment opportunity for Deaf Nepalis emerged in the late 1990s: employment in The Bakery Cafés. While working in tailoring typically signaled low-caste status, work in the food-service industry was associated with higher castes. This was because, as discussed previously, food was a highly salient means of transmitting substance in Nepal. Food exchanges were carefully managed, and most Nepalis paid close attention to the ritual status of those who prepared their food (Liechty 2001). Because, in food transactions, substance passed from the giver to the receiver, lower-caste persons could accept food or water from higher-caste individuals, but this directionality could not be reversed. As a consequence, many restaurants pointedly advertised that their staff members were all high caste.

However, customers did not necessarily believe such assurances; because of the impossibility of confirming the ritual status of all persons involved in preparing and serving the food, restaurants were often seen as dangerous sites. In fact, few restaurants existed in Nepal until after the country's borders were opened to foreigners. After Nepal became one of the first sites for U.S. Peace Corps volunteers in 1962, foreigners living in the country for extended periods created a demand for food-service establishments. These early restaurants were typically run by members of untouchable castes (the pie shops that were operated in an untouchable settlement that became known as Pie Alley were a well-known example) and therefore ritually out of bounds for most Kathmandu residents, especially upper-caste people, who were more likely to have been able to afford to eat out (Liechty 2001).

However, since the 1960s, in the public sphere of Kathmandu, a class-based logic of social relations had gradually been competing with and complicating one based on caste (Liechty 2001, 2003).[33] Within this framework, eating in restaurants, demonstrating that diners had cash to spend, became a way to show one's class identity. Additionally, eating in restaurants in which the ritual status of the employees was unknowable (despite assurances of their high-caste status from management) was also a means of displaying "modern" distance from the "backward" belief in ritual pollution (Liechty 2001). This background helps us understand the rationale behind and the effects of the Bakery Café's move to hire Deaf servers.

The Bakery Café credited itself on its website as having "introduced fast-food culture to the Kathmandu valley . . . the chain has been a key factor in cultivating a culture of eating out with friends, family, and colleagues." It further positioned itself as "today's favorite haunt for youngsters, families, and executives . . . eating at [the Bakery Café restaurants] is a noteworthy experience." The menus featured relatively high-priced fast food: burgers (buffalo rather than beef, in deference to the dominant Hindu population), fried chicken, and French fries, along with *thukpa* and *momos* (popular Tibetan noodle soup and dumplings, respectively) and other Nepali dishes. The atmosphere was explicitly designed to be perceived as modern and Western. For example, waitresses wore short skirts, while in the warm months the male servers wore shorts. Though fashion and standards for appropriate dress in Kathmandu were by no means static, in the 1990s and early 2000s such attire would have been seen as immodest and inappropriate in most contexts outside the restaurant.

The chain also advertised itself by saying, "the Bakery Café is known not only for its quality food, accessibility, and efficient service but also for

---

33. This shift in framework did not necessarily result in a change in the social actors advantaged: Although caste and class did not map onto one another perfectly, generally speaking, higher-caste persons were more likely to have more financial resources than lower-caste persons.

accepting and employing deaf staff." The Bakery Cafés began to feature Deaf waitstaff with the 1997 grand opening of its location in New Baneshwor, a relatively upscale neighborhood. I attended this festive event and often subsequently patronized the restaurant in order to visit with friends employed there. Several years later, in 2004, I interviewed Shyam Kakshapati, the Bakery Café owner who, in consultation with leaders of Nepal's associations of Deaf people, conceived of and executed the training of the Deaf waitstaff. Mr. Kakshapati was a member of the Rana family. As chapter 2 explains, the Ranas were hereditary prime ministers who ruled Nepal from 1846 to 1953. Though they kept Nepal isolated from outside influences, the members of the Rana family traveled extensively in Europe and were avid consumers of Western goods and ideas. This background may have influenced Kakshapati's project, as he had both financial resources and came from a family that maintained a long-standing engagement with Western institutions. Kakshapati himself, for example, was at one time well known for his Western hippie fashion sense.

While he collaborated in his project with leaders of associations of Deaf people and agreed to only hire Deaf servers fluent in NSL, in our interview and in his other discussions with the press, Kakshapati explicitly described his choice to hire Deaf servers in terms of engagement with disability rights. In this respect, the Bakery Café was distinct from its contemporaries, such as the Café Coffee Day (CCD) chain, a business in India that also made a point of hiring d/Deaf employees. The CCD explained its hiring decisions in terms of the benefits d/Deaf workers offered the business, claiming that they would be stable, long-term employees with a sense of gratitude for employment (Friedner 2013). Furthermore, the CCD regarded d/Deaf employees as "silent brewmasters," whose lack of hearing ostensibly heightened their coffee-making abilities. As "silent" figures, d/Deaf CCD employees did not directly engage with the public (Friedner 2013). Regarding the Bakery Café, Kakshapati had worried that, if he attempted to hide or even downplay the presence of his Deaf employees (by, for example, placing them in behind-the-scenes positions, such as dishwasher), his target (i.e., upper-middle-class) clientele might interpret this as a sign that the owner was "slumming it" by hiring inexpensive labor. Therefore, he decided that his best option was to be as open as possible about his decision to hire Deaf waitstaff, so that the business would not only function as, but also be seen as, a sort of development project.[34] Accordingly, the Deaf staff initially worked only in the highly visible role of waitstaff. Thus they were required to communicate directly with the (mostly hearing) clientele. How were these communicative interactions accomplished?

Reflecting and Producing Personhood in Ordering Interactions

My descriptions of engagements between Deaf waiters and hearing clientele in the Bakery Cafés draw on observations in the Jawalakhel and Thamel branches, which I frequented in 2001, 2004, and 2005. First, a word about these settings. The Jawalakhel outlet was in the city of Patan (one of the three former kingdoms of the Kathmandu Valley), known for housing many wealthy locals, foreign aid workers, and nongovernmental organization headquarters. Its Bakery Café was a popular meeting spot for foreign employees and volunteers, who congregated there after work. Local teenagers often came to use the computers in the upper level's "cyber kitchen." Local businessmen, upper-middle-class families, and foreign tourists also frequented the venue.

The Thamel café was in Kathmandu's primary tourist-oriented area (although the civil war had negatively affected tourism, it continued to be a mainstay of the economy). The neighborhood was composed mainly of both low- and high-budget hotels, bars, restaurants, and shops selling souvenirs, books, and trekking supplies. Many Nepalis considered this area as seedy and dangerous, in large part because it was a center for trade in illegal drugs. However, this image had made it popular with some younger, disaffected Nepali youth. Hanging out in Thamel allowed young Nepali men to claim a reputation as cool and tough. Even though in European and American contexts such affiliation is often associated with youth from lower-class backgrounds, in Nepal, to be a "tough guy" was a privilege associated with upper and middle classes (Liechty 2002).

These "punks," as they were locally called, were often, though not exclusively, well-educated but unable to find white-collar jobs. This frustration was a key component of their disaffection (ibid.). Police often harassed these

---

34. The Bakery Café was an entirely private-sector enterprise and did not receive funding from any government institutions. This echoed a broader trend in South Asia of shifting aid work from public to private entities.

punks, sometimes stopping them in the street and forcibly cutting off their long hair (a signature of the punk look in Nepal in the 1990s). (Several of my younger Deaf friends in Kathmandu identified themselves as punks; one, Chandeshwor, wore a baseball hat with a false ponytail attached in order to confound the police, who had previously shorn him in public.) Though punks were the Nepali youth initially most likely to spend time in Thamel, in the mid-2000s, sites such as the Thamel Bakery Café and nearby coffee shops had become popular with middle-class youths who had not adopted a punk persona but had embraced modern consumer practices. Both groups gravitated to what they perceived to be Western culture, often viewed wistfully as existing in distant centers while they themselves remained "out here" in peripheral Kathmandu (Liechty 2002). In sum, the clientele at each of these branches included primarily foreigners (e.g., aid workers, tourists) and upper-class Nepalis (e.g., businessmen, youths engaging in modern consumerism).

When the Bakery Cafés first introduced Deaf servers at each venue, the management took pains to provide customers with explicit instructions for interacting with the waiters. Each table was outfitted with a notice explaining the "special" nature of the waitstaff and informing patrons that the café was participating in the social betterment of d/Deaf people. The notices thus implied that a "modernity and development" framework, rather than one based on notions of ritual pollution, should guide customers in their interactions with the servers. At the same time, however, these notices were decorated with *mudras* (hand positions conveying complex meanings found in Hindu and Buddhist iconographic sculpture and painting), which served to frame hand gestures in a positive rather than a negative religious light.

In the early years the text on these notices made it clear that customers were not expected to engage in signing or gesturing with the waiters. Rather, it was suggested that they place their orders by pointing to the desired items on the menu. The menu text was in English, which was itself often associated with modernity and therefore allowed a modern language and modality (writing) to mediate between the interlocutors. By making these choices in creating the menu, the management presupposed both patrons and servers who were literate in English (and who, having likely learned this skill in school, were likely well educated and from higher-class backgrounds).

How did customers respond? In order not to disrupt business I did not interview customers in the Bakery Cafés but rather observed interactions.

In the early years of Deaf employment at the Bakery Cafés I sometimes overheard hearing patrons, once seated at their table, discuss the notice. Sometimes they made jokes along the lines of "Well, at least we know they won't eavesdrop on our conversation!" Sometimes they imagined the mishaps that could occur, considering that not all of the employees in a given branch were Deaf. How, couples frequently speculated, would one know, when initiating an interaction, whether one's interlocutor was deaf or hearing? Typically, when first approaching a table, a Deaf waitperson would signal his or her status by greeting the patrons with a namaste. This gesture, illustrated in figure 13 by a screenshot from the Bakery Café commercial mentioned at the beginning of the chapter, involved pressing the palms of the hands together. Hearing Nepalis routinely performed this gesture of greeting as well, typically accompanying it with the spoken word "namaste"; the silent, and often slightly exaggerated, performance of a namaste suggested a waitperson's Deaf status. Once realizing that a given waitperson was deaf, many customers would restrict their interactions with the server to pointing at the menu text and did not further use gesture as a resource to expand the interactions. If some elaboration were required (for example, when an adjustment to an order was necessary), customers frequently sought a hearing host or manager with whom to discuss the matter.

Sites such as TripAdvisor, which have emerged in recent years as forums in which customers rate restaurants and hotels, provide insight into clients' explicit reflections on the experience of ordering from Deaf waiters. Comments on such sites sometimes mention communication difficulties caused by the presence of Deaf waiters. For example, a commenter from Kathmandu wrote, "We were on the way to Changu Narayan [a temple] and thought to have breakfast. So we rushed to the Bakery Café of New Baneshwor where the dumb and deft [sic] were there. It was really difficult for us to order what we wanted to have. Even though we had faced difficulty to communicate, the service was excellent."[35] More frequently, however, such comments report experiences of communicative ease. For

---

35. mdkiran, comment on Bakery Café, *TripAdvisor*, September 18, 2012, http://www.tripadvisor.com/ShowUserReviews-g293890-d1154225-r146959816-Bakery_Cafe-Kathmandu_Kathmandu_Valley_Bagmati_Zone_Central_Region.html.

Figure 13

example, two other commenters wrote that, "The Bakery Café hires wait-staff who are hearing impaired, so you should expect that they will want you to point to the item on the menu when you order. If there is any question, they will get the guy with good hearing to come out and clarify."[36] Another noted that "Communication is often done via smiles and nods, which make it a very warm and welcoming environment, but no need to fear, if you do have any questions about the food/menu or have any dietary restrictions there are people there who you can speak to directly."[37]

The success of Kakshapati's initiative was reflected in the expansion of the program from twelve Deaf waiters at the initial New Baneshwor outlet

---

36. Joe N, comment on Bakery Café, *TripAdvisor*, May 4, 2013, http://www.tripadvisor.com/ShowUserReviews-g315764-d1156662-r167667748-Bakery_Cafe-Patan_Lalitpur_Kathmandu_Valley_Bagmati_Zone_Central_Region.html.

37. Andree R, comment on Bakery Café, *TripAdvisor*, April 2, 2012, http://www.tripadvisor.com/ShowUserReviews-g315764-d1156662-r159588715-Bakery_Cafe-Patan_Lalitpur_Kathmandu_Valley_Bagmati_Zone_Central_Region.html.

in 1997, to forty-five Deaf servers (25 percent of the chain's total workers) in eight Kathmandu outlets by 2010. This success was also reflected in a shift over time in how hearing customers engaged with the Deaf waitstaff. Although the online reviewers quoted earlier stressed that it was possible to use written or spoken language in ordering, between 1997 and 2006 I observed that customers increasingly began to draw on their gestural repertoires to both place orders and expand their interactions with the waiters.

Indeed, many co-speech gestures were widely used in Nepal, and a number of these had been incorporated into both homesign systems and NSL. For example, I had been taught NOT/NO in my initial NSL lessons before I noticed the ubiquitous use of a similar gesture among hearing Nepalis. One day, when I approached an army gasoline pump on my scooter, I found myself confronted by a soldier wearing army fatigues and vigorously making what I understood as NOT/NO in NSL to indicate, from a distance, that there was no gasoline available that day. At first I was taken aback and wondered whether the soldier might know NSL or be Deaf, but soon I realized that the form of the sign overlapped with a widely used gesture that also indicated negation.

Thus, Bakery Café clients often did not need to venture far out of their existing gestural repertoire to expand such interactions. Nevertheless, the hearing clients sometimes treated these exchanges as amusing, as they laughingly dissected the interaction after an order had been placed. However, for regular customers, the act of using gesture to place an order often came to feel more natural. In response to this shift, the Bakery Café began efforts to popularize lexical items from NSL that hearing people could use in ordering particular menu items. Television advertisements introduced the wider public to these signs, including BURGER (see figure 14), COFFEE, MOMO, PIZZA, TEA, and DOSA (a South Indian crepe-like dish). TripAdvisor comments began, after this era, to mention the possibility of communicating with the waitstaff via signs. For example, one reviewer wrote that, "If you want to show appreciation smile or learn sign language for 'thank you' "[38]). Another enthused that they, "got enlightened by the

---

38. Allid64, comment on Bakery Cafe, *TripAdvisor*, April 7, 2013, http://www.tripadvisor.com/ShowUserReviews-g293890-d1154225-r160019491-Bakery_Cafe-Kathmandu_Kathmandu_Valley_Bagmati_Zone_Central_Region.html.

Figure 14

gestures and means of communication with referral to various food stuffs by these amazing set of people !!! amazing experience !!"[39]

Reflecting and affecting the increasing popularity of this practice, in 2008 the Nepali pop star Yogeshwor (Yogi) Amatya released a music video filmed at the Bakery Café. The video, for the song "Kya Bore Bhayo" ("What a Bore"), incorporated Deaf waiters into its story line and used them as actors. The (fictional) plot involves a Deaf Bakery Café waitress who has a crush on a hearing patron. Her longing for him to show up at the restaurant during her shift constitutes the "bore" referred to in the title. The object of her affection, in a Western suit and sunglasses, exemplifies a high-class, bikāsi persona. During the video, however, it becomes clear that the customer is instead interested in another hearing patron, an attractive young woman who has been

39. Sachin90, comment on Bakery Café, *TripAdvisor,* July 3, 2015, http://www. tripadvisor.com/ShowUserReviews-g293890-d777284-r321534256-The_Bakery_Cafe-Kathmandu_Kathmandu_Valley_Bagmati_Zone_Central_Region.html.

eyeing him across the café. To the waitress's distress, the hearing couple begins to have dates at the restaurant.[40] The video ends by suggesting that, though the Deaf waitress could not have her wish for romance with the wealthy hearing customer, a fellow Deaf waiter has romantic feelings for her. In this respect, even as the video promoted "modern" practices such as engaging in romantic dating in public, it reinforced the idea that people should ultimately pair up with partners from their own jāt, in this respect reinforcing the notion of an endogamous Deaf jāt (chapter 3).

The video included many shots of Deaf servers using NSL to talk to one another, as well as footage of the customers using gesture and occasionally signs to attract the attention of the waitstaff and to place orders. The fictionalized interactions between hearing and Deaf characters were not plagued by any issues of miscommunication, except for one scene in which the Deaf waitress failed to respond to a customer's attempt to get her attention; however, the video implied that this was not because she was deaf but because she was preoccupied with gazing at the front door in the hope that her crush would enter.

In between scenes showing this love story playing out in the Bakery Café, the video cut to shots of Yogeshwor Amatya singing. Amatya's performance consisted of occasional NSL signs embedded in the emotive, idiosyncratic gestures for which he was well known. He distinctly signed BHAYO ("happened") in Nepali, mapping it onto his spoken utterance of the term in the chorus: *kya bore bhayo,* literally, "what (a) bore (has) happened" (in idiomatic English, "What a bore!"). This sign was not typically incorporated into Deaf signing practice but was derived from the Signed Nepali practices used by (and with) many

---

40. The Bakery Café was in fact a popular location for young people on dates (skating the ever-changing edge of propriety during the time of my fieldwork) and was a favorite place to celebrate Valentine's Day, a holiday that was new to Nepal in the 1990s and early 2000s but was becoming popular with middle- and upper-class youth. On Valentine's Day in 2005, for example, I spent the afternoon with several Deaf employees of the Bakery Café, who were anticipating their shift that evening with trepidation, as they expected to be kept at work quite late due to an onslaught of customers.

hearing signers.[41] Amatya also frequently performed a movement that resembled DRUNK or ALCOHOL in NSL. This may have been an inside joke as the performer's popular persona was one of benign dissipation (when giving interviews, he frequently stressed that his favorite activity in the world was to drink beer and whiskey at a bar late into the night).

Though there were very few traces of NSL in his performance, and even though dramatic gestures were his signature style, many viewers of the "Kya Bore Bhayo" video interpreted Amatya's movements as a simultaneous performance of sung Nepali and signed NSL. For example, hearing Nepali friends of mine, aware of my research interests, have directed my attention to the video in which "the singer uses sign language." The comment threads associated with the video's appearance on YouTube echo this sentiment. For example, one poster wrote, "Did anyone notice!!!! he is actually singing for hearing loss people as well . . . he is using sign language! Good job."[42] It is quite likely that this was the impression those who created the video wished viewers to form.

Why did a hearing pop singer incorporate Deaf waitstaff into a music video and position himself as someone using sign language, and why was he congratulated for doing so? Why did the Bakery Café create commercials encouraging customers to use NSL signs when ordering despite the fact that it had been established that doing so was not necessary? The use of NSL signs by hearing persons indicated greater social engagement with the d/Deaf persons, with the effects on hearing persons that this, in turn, might produce: Specifically, eating in a Bakery Café and signing with a Deaf waitperson could, in addition to signaling a request for, say, a burger, both reflect and produce modern and bikāsi qualities in the hearing person.

This was accomplished in part by the owners' efforts to align the Bakery Café with development projects. This meant that customers could, by

---

41. More specifically (and likely inadvertently), he used the Signed Nepali term that was developed to represent the Nepali word *hunubhayo*, a construction that denotes "happened" but does so in a way that indicates a higher level of respect toward the subject of the verb than *bhayo* alone conveys.

42. Saurav ojha, comment on "Kya Bore Bhayo" video, *YouTube*, 2009, https://www.youtube.com/watch?v=uHbaiCnPzuM.

ordering food in an expensive restaurant, see themselves as actively participating in the development of d/Deaf people. Indeed, comments on review
websites such as TripAdvisor, from both locals and customers from abroad,
typically portrayed the Bakery Café in this light. Even though customers might post complaints about the food (its expense or blandness), they
generally followed such comments with assertions that it was nevertheless
worthwhile to eat there in order to support the "good work" the restaurants
were doing. For example, a visitor from Singapore described the Bakery
Café as "a café employing people who are less than ordinary, mostly with
[a] hearing and speaking handicap, another reason to patronize the café,
besides their reasonable food."[43] A customer from New Zealand wrote,
"The waiters at this place are deaf/dumb, which I thought was very good
of the management,"[44] while a commenter from Scotland wrote that, "In
a city as developing as Kathmandu [it] was fantastic to see a place where
deaf Nepalis are given the opportunity to provide a first class service."[45] A
poster from Kathmandu wrote that is was, "Good to go eat and support
the deaf employing cause."[46]

That travelers from abroad viewed themselves as participating in a
development initiative through their purchasing power is not surprising.
However, the Nepali customers' patronage of the restaurants allowed them
to occupy the position of modern and bikāsi aid giver frequently denied
them in global discourses that frame Nepalis as perpetual receivers of aid.
Furthermore, for Nepali customers, these social meanings and effects

43. Lyefei, comment on Bakery Café, *TripAdvisor,* October 12, 2013, http://
www.tripadvisor.com/ShowUserReviews-g315764-d1156662-r187227093-Bakery_
Cafe-Patan_Lalitpur_Kathmandu_Valley_Bagmati_Zone_Central_Region.html.

44. shanzx, comment on Bakery Café, *TripAdvisor*, September 29, 2009, http://
www.tripadvisor.com/ShowUserReviews-g315764-d1156662-r124185715-
Bakery_Cafe-Patan_Lalitpur_Kathmandu_Valley_Bagmati_Zone_Central_
Region.html.

45. Clare Q, comment on Bakery Café, *TripAdvisor*, May 9, 2013, http://www.
tripadvisor.com/ShowUserReviews-g315764-d1156662-r160154401-Bakery_
Cafe-Patan_Lalitpur_Kathmandu_Valley_Bagmati_Zone_Central_Region.html.

46. Ashok S, comment on Bakery Café, *TripAdvisor*, November 16, 2014, http://
www.tripadvisor.com/Restaurant_Review-g315764-d1156662-Reviews-Bakery_
Cafe-Patan_Lalitpur_Kathmandu_Valley_Bagmati_Zone_Central_Region.html.

emerged not just from alignment with Western development practices but also because they publicly rejected the notion that d/Deaf persons transmitted ritual pollution; eating in the Bakery Café was a very explicit way of publicly displaying "modern" disregard for such concerns. Thus, Deaf employees were represented as nonpolluting in a way that simultaneously evoked (in order to reject) the idea (against which the associations of Deaf people had struggled) that they were ritually polluted.

Rules about ritual pollution were flouted for particular social effects in other contexts as well. For example, as discussed in chapter 2, it was against the rules of commensality to eat food off someone else's plate after that person had begun to eat from it. The food would be *juṭho,* ritually impure. However, parents sometimes ate food polluted by their children's prior tastings as a way to express intimacy. The effects of this act were facilitated by the rules that were being broken: If there was no proscription against eating off the child's plate, it would not be possible to produce intimacy by breaking the rule (Parish 1994, 154). Likewise, should belief in ritual pollution become less socially significant in Nepal or should d/Deafness cease to be associated with ritual pollution, neither the negative (generating pollution) nor the positive (generating bikāsi) effects on hearing interlocutors who engage with d/Deaf people might persist (or persist in the same way).

Thus, though the Bakery Café's use of Deaf servers functioned to reduce some of the stigma of d/Deafness in Kathmandu, it also depicted the Deaf waiters as being "undeveloped" aid recipients, an attribute often globally associated with all Nepalis. In so doing, it promoted a disability rather than an ethnolinguistic model of the nature of d/Deafness. Consequently, just as many d/Deaf Café Coffee Day workers were ambivalent about the company's practice of hiring deaf servers (Friedner 2013), it is possible that Deaf Nepali employees were likewise critical of the Bakery Café. However, over the course of my research none of them voiced such concerns to me. This may have been in order to avoid jeopardizing their employment. However, many of my research participants explicitly expressed their pleasure at having a job where Deaf sociality was possible—an important difference between the Bakery Café and the Café Coffee Day (the latter had a policy of placing only a single d/Deaf employee in a given outlet) or the Swedish Sewing Project, which focused on returning Deaf tailors to their natal villages and hearing networks.

Bakery Cafés and Deaf Tourism

Furthermore, sociality between employees was not the only type of Deaf relationships these restaurants facilitated. The Bakery Cafés increasingly attracted d/Deaf as well as hearing tourists from abroad, including those who specifically wished to connect with what is sometimes called the "Deaf-World" (often indicated by DEAF DEAF SAME, a notion of Deaf similitude that transcends "geography, culture, space, and time" [Friedner and Kusters 2014, 2]). This concept stresses not only presumed similarities in Deaf signers' experiences around the world (e.g., the use of a sign language and the experience of being part of a cultural and linguistic minority group) but also the linguistic and cultural diversity associated with Deafness (as neither sign languages nor practices associated with "Deaf culture" are universal). In recent years emerging tourism businesses run by Deaf entrepreneurs have made use of the Deaf-World trope in order to offer formal travel services that facilitate Deafcentric tourism as a way to explore these similarities and differences. For example, the company Discovering Deaf Worlds (DDS) has led group tours to a wide range of countries, and its website advertises "culture, adventure, accessibility, and a way to engage with international Deaf communities."

On my 2015 research trip to Nepal (one of the DDS destinations, in fact), it was indeed clear that it had become a popular destination for Deaf tourism. This can be partly attributed to the many attractions (e.g., Mount Everest, trekking, temples, tigers) that have made tourism the country's largest industry. Additionally, Deaf social networks in Nepal have increasingly become known abroad for being particularly robust and organized around Deafcentric spaces such as associations of Deaf people and residential schools for d/Deaf children. Due to factors such as mainstreaming and cochlear implantation, the prevalence of such centers has declined in Euro-America in recent decades. As a result, some Deaf signers from these regions express nostalgia for a Deaf social life centered around such institutions.

The Bakery Cafés were a popular site for Deaf tourists who wish to meet local Deaf signers. Other businesses that advertised and catered specifically to Deaf visitors have also emerged. For example, on our 2015 visit to Nepal my students and I stayed for several weeks at the Hotel Metropolitan Kantipur, owned and run by the Shakya family, including

Pramila and Devendra Shakya, a Deaf married couple. During our stay there my students and I met and socialized with d/Deaf guests from five different countries (and this was during the winter monsoon, definitely the off-season for tourism in Nepal). Many Deaf Nepalis (including my friend Pramod, mentioned in chapter 2) had established travel guide and trekking businesses specifically geared to d/Deaf visitors.

Interactions between Deaf Nepalis and d/Deaf tourists from abroad have the potential to confirm, challenge, or reconstruct participants' understandings of the nature of a Deaf-World, including its centers and its peripheries.[47] Although, as mentioned earlier, Nepal has often been understood as being on the global periphery in geographic, political, and economic terms, its retention of important Deafcentric institutions may allow signers to perceive it instead as a center in a Deaf-World. At the same time, the nation's marginal status in the hearing world remains relevant, as Deaf visitors from politically and economically dominant countries have often been afforded resources and travel opportunities (e.g., the ability to visit other nations as a tourist) that tended to be less accessible to Nepali citizens, including Deaf Nepalis.

In conclusion, this chapter has focused on additional ideological frameworks and sets of reflective and creative social indexicalities invoked when hearing Nepalis interacted with Deaf servers in Bakery Cafés. As the final discussion of Deaf tourism indicates, however, the ideological and indexical processes that affect and are affected by social relations vary widely according to differently positioned sets of interactants. This increases the complexity of the webs of significance through which persons and broader groups are coproduced. This complexity in turn affects and is affected by changes over time. The final chapter addresses such historical contingency by exploring events after Nepal's transition to a secular republic.

---

47. For example, Deaf travelers from the "global North" may imagine the Deaf networks in the "global South" as "deaf heavens or hells" as they make sense of their experiences or justify their interventions in those places (Friedner and Kusters 2014, 1). These impressions go both ways, of course; Pratigya Shakya's series of grotesque paintings of the effects of cochlear implantation suggests a view of the global North as itself hellish for d/Deaf people.

Deaf in a "New Nepal"

6

IN JANUARY 2015, I visited Nepal for the first time after an unusually lengthy absence. My long-standing pattern of returning to conduct research or visit friends at least every other year had been disrupted by the demands of both parenthood and being on the tenure track. During my briefer absences from the country in the 1990s and early 2000s, Deaf friends and I had communicated primarily by letter, a medium that yielded mementos I still treasure but which required that we use written English or Nepali rather than the NSL that we relied on in person. The increasingly widespread availability of the Internet fortunately co-occurred with my extended absence, enabling us to video-chat using NSL and observe the intimate details of our everyday lives as posted to Facebook on a daily basis. As mentioned in chapter 1, many newer Deaf friends associated the form of my name sign with EMAIL, and though this did not accurately reflect the historical emergence of my name sign, this interpretation of its possible iconic and indexical motivations did accurately reflect a current social reality.

Though letters, Facebook, and Skype had allowed us to follow the details of one another's lives, whether mundane or exceptional, it was something else to finally be together again in person. With the cheerful bluntness characteristic of Nepalis in general, most of my friends greeted me with lengthy descriptions of how OLD and FAT I had become and laughed good naturedly when I returned the "compliments." Reflecting on our physical changes, we talked at length about the events, both personal (family and career) and national (historical and political changes since 2006), that had precipitated them.

Awareness of how Deaf Nepalis' lives have changed over time, accessible only through the long-term relationships that make longitudinal ethnographic research possible, allows me to assess and update the claims I've made in this book (see Tetreault [forthcoming] for a broader discussion of long-term ethnographic research). In particular, such changes explain how the processes, ideologies, and relations described in this book related to the particular historical period I had studied. That is not to say that, in Nepal, Deaf social life was determined by this setting but rather that Deaf Nepalis were responsive to the contexts in which NSL and Deaf social networks had emerged and grown. The responsiveness of Deaf Nepalis has continued as the political structure of Nepal has changed since the end of the "People's War."

A New Nepal

In the spring of 2006, soon after I had returned to the United States from the last of my dissertation research trips, the Jana Adolan 2 ousted the Nepali king and brought about the end of the war. In 2008, a Constituent Assembly was elected to function as an interim legislature and to draft a new constitution for what was often referred to as a nāya Nepal ("new Nepal"). For the first time in such a position, the assembly included a Deaf member: Raghav Bir Joshi. The Maoists, who had been reincorporated into the government in the form of the United Communist Party of Nepal (Maoist) (CPN[M]) won the greatest number of seats. On its first meeting, the Constituent Assembly declared Nepal a secular democratic republic. However, the assembly was dissolved in 2012 due to its failure to produce a constitution.

One of the primary points of contention preventing the framing of a new constitution had been disagreement about how such a document should both address and redress the long-standing inequalities between social groups in Nepal (Hangen 2007). Since the beginning of the war, the Maoists had proposed the formation of autonomous regions in Nepal, structured along ethnic lines, as a means of overturning the preceding centuries of marginalization of lower-caste and ethnic groups (Lawoti 2005; Mirsha and Gurung 2012; Rai 2013). As the CPN(M), they continued to advocate this approach for restructuring the government. Ādivāsi janajāti groups, which emerged from the war as important political actors, also demanded that the new constitution incorporate ethnic federalism and outlined specific proposals for ethnic autonomous regions based on their readings of how ethnic identity and history mapped onto territory (Lawoti 2013). Similarly, Madhesi groups (castes and "tribal" groups from the southern Terai region), demanded "one Madhesh, one Pradesh," the formation of a single federal state encompassing the Terai region.

Older political parties represented in the Constituent Assemblies largely agreed that Nepal's government had been overly centralized but argued for administrative rather than ethnic federalism. In resisting ethnic federalism many politicians argued that discrete and homogeneous ethnic groups do not neatly map onto discrete and homogeneous territories, claiming that in some cases different ethnic groups have each claimed a right to control the same territory (Hangen 2007). This critical assessment of an understanding of ethnicities as monolithic and discrete is a departure from previous tactics of the state. Indeed, in earlier periods, state consolidation and recognition of ethnic categories had been important features of Nepali governance. During that earlier "classificatory moment," however, the creation and deployment of jāt categories was driven by the state in order "to codify hierarchy within a Hindu ideological frame that enabled exploitation of certain groups by others" (Shneiderman 2013, 44).

Conversely, mainstream political parties viewed ethnic groups' efforts to self-categorize as threatening. In particular, though the state's previous efforts to reify ethnic categories were framed as unifying, mainstream parties argued that ethnic federalism would fracture the nation. Anthropologists studying this political debate note that, although there are indeed important complications and concerns regarding the implementation of ethnic federalism, it is also necessary to critically examine how the dominant political discourse employs a politics of fear to "mute and marginalize the multiple indigenous federal imaginations from meaningful public debates in Nepal" (Rai 2013, 339; Shneiderman 2013).

In 2013, a second Constituent Assembly was elected with a mandate to choose a course of action regarding federalism and to produce a new constitution by January 22, 2015. As my most recent research trip to Nepal coincided with this deadline and the weeks leading up to it, my students and I were able to observe the series of *bandas* (strikes), through which parties with competing interests sought to encourage lawmakers to either meet or resist the deadline. Ultimately, the deadline passed without a new constitution.

Land and Language

How did Deaf Nepalis respond to this shifting political field following the transition to a secular republic? As my research into this question is ongoing, I offer the following observations less in order to make a strong argument about the current and future state of affairs and more to nuance our understanding of the preceding ethnographic moments that this book explores. Throughout this book I have argued that the adoption of an ethnolinguistic framing of Deafness potentially aligned Deaf Nepalis with other marginalized ethnic groups during the war. I have outlined the language standardization processes through which leaders of the national associations of Deaf people sought to make NSL and a Deaf jāt appear uniform and therefore recognizable to their government and to international organizations. In so doing, I have explored both how this process replicated the hegemonic discourses of the state and how Deaf signers navigated the internal hierarchies that this form of standardization produced (Shneiderman 2013). However, with changes to the political structure in Nepal have come changes in these alignments, ideologies, and practices.

For example, as the preceding brief discussion of the post-2006 political scene suggests, struggles over the question of ethnic federalism both reflected and affected a "heightened sense" of "geographical imagination" (Harvey 2005, 212, cited in Rai 2013, 16) among Nepal's marginalized communities (see also Tamang 2009). That is not to say that issues surrounding language were no longer relevant to ādivāsi janajāti, Dalit, or Madhesi politics but rather that territorial claims had superseded them in the context of debates over a new constitution. Territory, however, had not been a particularly relevant component of the constitution of a Deaf jāt. Thus, the strength of the alignment between Deaf Nepalis and other politically active marginalized ethnic groups seems to have decreased in the postwar period.

Additionally, although the structural inequalities embedded in Nepali governance have been less tractable in the forging of a "new Nepal," symbolic changes have occurred fairly readily (Hangen 2007). For example, in 2007 the national anthem was changed from "Rastriya Gān," a song praising the Hindu king, to "Sayaun Thunga Phul Ka" ("Made of Hundreds of Flowers"). The new anthem concludes with a line that can be translated as "of many races, languages, religions, and cultures of incredible sprawl, this progressive nation of ours, all hail Nepal," indicating a desire to achieve a (still imagined) multicultural republic not hierarchically organized according to the Hindu caste system.[48] Thus, just as the claim of NSL as a mother

---

48. As opposed to Prithvi Narayan Shah's hierarchical "garden" of castes.

tongue may no longer have as clearly aligned Deaf Nepalis with politically active ethnic groups, so the processes of sanskritization enacted by efforts to standardize NSL had become a less effective way to align with the symbols of the state.

I can provide only preliminary but nonetheless telling anecdotal observations of how these broader changes have affected signing practice in Deaf networks. Throughout my most recent research trip, I frequently noticed friends using signs with which I was unfamiliar. It is hardly surprising that this would be the case. Given that, as is the case for all languages, NSL is neither homogeneous nor unchanging, and given that my friends had diverse linguistic repertoires, I would not expect to find their signing practice completely unchanged after my absence. Whenever I encountered an unfamiliar sign, I asked for its meaning and usually also received some account of what the signer understood to be its provenance. Some signs were identified as ASL or International Sign (IS). Indeed, in a study of sociolinguistic variation in NSL, Khanal (2013b, 12) notes that Deaf youth in the Thamel (tourist) area of Kathmandu were using numerous borrowed signs, which both reflected and affected their relationships with international Deaf visitors.

However, some changes suggested that an ideological shift was under way. These included not only the appearance of different elements in signers' repertoires but also the contexts in which they performed these different elements, as well as the ways in which they discussed or reacted to them. For example, readers may recall that in chapter 3 I described how uncomfortable my friend Jitendra had been with his wife's family's former homesign for "mother." In 2005 he had been deeply reluctant to perform the sign, which traced the shape of a breast, even in the context of explaining that he had succeeded in eliminating its use in the household. Therefore, while spending time with him in 2015, I was startled to notice variants of this sign appearing in his conversation whenever he referred to women in general or to particular types of females (such as mothers or wives). This occurred frequently and regardless of whether we were at events that were oriented more to Deaf groups (e.g., a party with all Deaf friends) or kin networks (e.g., a big family picnic). Not wanting to make him uncomfortable, I did not remind him of his previous stance toward this homesign but simply asked him about its meaning. He replied that it referred to women and could be adapted to provide more specificity. "Is it an NSL sign or a natural sign?" I asked. "No, no," he replied, "it is a Newar sign."

What did this mean? On previous research trips, friends had often indicated that certain natural signs (or, as I have been referring to them in this book, homesigns) were grounded in specifically Newar practices (recall, for example, when Jagajeet offered me an impromptu evening lesson in some homesigns used in his Newar networks in Kirtipur [chapter 4]). Indeed, as Newars were the largest ādivāsi janajāti group in the Kathmandu Valley, it was not surprising that homesigns indexing Newarness were often the foils against which NSL and a Deaf jāt were made distinctive. By 2015, however, it seemed that nonstandard signs that could index Newar jāt membership were being labeled not as natural signs but Newar signs; in other words, they were treated as a distinct variety of signing.

Not only were these labeling practices changing, but so were the contexts in which people performed these signs. I previously explained that many signers used the standard NSL lexicon in institutions for Deaf persons and switched to homesigns in kinship networks. However, in 2015, I frequently observed Newar signs being both used and labeled as such in sites of Deaf sociality. This may have been in part because boundaries between contexts for Deaf and kinship sociality had become blurrier; as more cohorts of Deaf signers had married one another, and as work and family obligations kept them busy and less able to spend time at the associations of Deaf people, they increasingly made their homes sites for Deaf social life. The porousness of the previously more tightly maintained boundaries between these social spaces may have reflected and perpetuated a similar blurring of the boundaries between NSL and particular sets of homesigns, yielding a new label for variation in linguistic repertoires: Newar signs.

These changes suggest changes in progress with regard to how Deaf Nepalis manage the relationships between the different jāt categories to which they belong. In future research I will continue to explore this topic.

Conclusions

This book has sought to complicate a common narrative in the literature about young or emerging sign languages and d/Deaf social networks. Such work has typically stressed a transition from diversity (many idiosyncratic homesign systems) to convergence—unified sign languages mapped onto likewise unified Deaf communities (often, though not exclusively, themselves mapped onto national boundaries). However, although shared practices of performing and interpreting signs are indeed important resources for networks of Deaf signers, this book has shown that such convergence is not produced through the absence of difference. Rather, variation in producing and interpreting signs is itself an important means of generating social personas, activities, and categories (including the notion of distinct languages). Indeed, just as I have argued that persons and larger social formations can be mutually constituted through interaction, difference and likeness are likewise mutually productive.

It is not possible to understand how people perceive, make sense of, and attempt to reduce or produce differences and similarities in language use without accounting for the broader social, historical, and ideological contexts in which linguistic interactions take place (and which they both reflect and affect). In examining the articulation of NSL and a Deaf jāt during the period of the Maoist People's War, I have sought to move away from the tendency of some Deaf studies (e.g., Lane et al. 1996; Lane 2005) to universalize members of a Deaf-World as "unmarked, unemplaced, dehierarchized, and ungendered" (Friedner and Kusters 2014, 5). Such an ideological stance has consequences. When adopted by national and international organizations of Deaf persons promoting an ethnolinguistic model of Deafness, their focus on establishing and supporting national associations of Deaf persons and encouraging the codification of national sign languages can erase or problematize linguistic and social diversity among the d/Deaf signers within a national boundary (ibid., 12). Indeed, in adopting a linguistic monolith perspective in the project to standardize NSL, Nepal's associations of Deaf people responded not only to their local ideological context but also to language ideologies broadly circulated by international organizations of Deaf persons.

However, as this book has illustrated, a linguistic monolith framework for understanding language is neither adequate nor all encompassing. In contexts in which this ideology dominates, even when characterized as a problem, linguistic and social diversity continue to exist and function as resources for generating meaning and forging relations. Nor is a linguistic monolith understanding of the nature of languages inevitable or universal. Its wide circulation during the period this book describes is itself both responsive to and productive of a particular historical moment. Such moments change, and this book, at its core, has been a study of the processes through which social change occurs. Ultimately, I hope to have shown that Deaf Nepalis will continue not only to respond to local and transnational changes but also to be agents in producing such change.

Afterword

On April 25, 2015, a massive earthquake shook Nepal. As I completed this manuscript in early May of that year, the death count was continuing to rise. The Kathmandu Valley, the primary site of my research for this book and where most of my Nepali friends live, was devastated. Rural areas were hit even harder. As I write, Nepalis in both urban areas and villages are still awaiting relief from the government or aid groups. Countless Nepalis are now without safe homes in which to take shelter from the incipient monsoon season.

Through a stroke of great luck, the Kathmandu Association of the Deaf was holding its annual Nepali New Year's picnic when the earthquake struck on a sunny Saturday afternoon. Thus many of its members were gathered in an open area, away from buildings that could have crushed them. However, some Deaf Nepalis in the Kathmandu Valley were injured, and many have lost homes and other property. Word is only now starting to come in from more remote regions, where the status of rural associations and schools for Deaf persons has been unknown.

As I alternate between obsessively checking Facebook for updates on both individual friends and the situation broadly, organizing fund-raising events, and finalizing this manuscript, I have noticed a change in how I interpret some of my stylistic choices while writing this book. In particular, I have been careful always to use the past tense in order to make it clear that I am not making generalized claims about a timeless Nepali Sign Language or Deaf social life in Nepal but rather providing an ethnographic account of a particular historical moment. Many of the processes and beliefs I describe here are, in fact, ongoing today, but, as chapter 6 begins to explain, others have changed. Who knows what further changes will have occurred by the time this book is read in the future?

However, as I reread my manuscript in the immediate wake of the earthquake, my use of the past tense seems less to imply an awareness of potential changes and more to invoke a sense of loss. Nonetheless, despite the unimaginable scale of the earthquake's destruction, it is also clear that Nepalis, including Deaf Nepalis, will rebuild their damaged structures, heritage, and networks of relationships. Madhu, the elderly Deaf man described in chapter 4, was alive when the last major earthquake struck Nepal in 1934, and he has often described the experience of being injured in the event. At that time, as in 2015, much of Nepal, including the beautiful cities of the Kathmandu Valley, was destroyed—and later rebuilt. Therefore, without minimizing or discounting the irreplaceable lost lives and terrible suffering that is ongoing, I join my Nepali friends and colleagues in imagining and working for not only reconstruction but also new possibilities.

In particular, many Nepalis have been frustrated by the fact that the "new Nepal" expected after the end of the war has been slow in coming. The earthquake has disproportionately affected those Nepalis who were politically, socially, and economically marginalized both before and after the war. The aftermath of the earthquake may continue to exacerbate their marginalization, but this moment of disruption may also have the potential to reconfigure these relations. Pratigya Shakya, the Deaf Nepali artist whose work has frequently appeared in this book, has been recording and circulating online a series of videos in which he shows viewers in the Deaf-World (to which he specifically refers) the damage to his city, but he also draws (sometimes in chalk right in front of a damaged site) a projected, re-created Nepal. He has asserted in these videos that Nepal can be "made new," a multivalent phrase that can suggest re-creation as well as reproduction. I join him in this hope.

Bibliography

Acharya, Kiran. 1997. *A History of the Deaf in Nepal*, translated by Erika Hoffmann and Dambar Chemjong in 2004. Kathmandu: National Association of the Deaf and Hard of Hearing.

Ahearn, Laura. 2001. *Invitations to Love: Literacy, Love Letters, and Social Change in Nepal*. Ann Arbor: University of Michigan Press.

Ahearn, Laura. 2012. *Living Language: An Introduction to Linguistic Anthropology*. Malden, MA: Wiley-Blackwell.

Alonso, Ana Maria. 1994. The Politics of Space, Time and Substance: State Formation, Nationalism and Ethnicity. *Annual Review of Anthropology* 23: 379–405.

Bailey, Benjamin. 1997. Communication of Respect in Interethnic Service Encounters. *Language in Society* 26(3): 327–56.

Bakhtin, Mikhail. 1981. *The Dialogic Imagination: Four Essays*. Edited by Michael Holquist. Translated by Caryl Emerson, and Michael Holquist. Austin: University of Texas Press.

Barth, Fredrick. 1969. Introduction. In *Ethnic Groups and Boundaries: The Social Organization of Cultural Difference*, edited by Fredrick Barth, 9–38. Boston: Little, Brown.

Baynton, Douglas. 1996. *Forbidden Signs: American Culture and the Campaign against Sign Language*. Chicago: University of Chicago Press.

———. 2008. Beyond Culture: Deaf Studies and the Deaf Body. In *Open Your Eyes: Deaf Studies Talking*, edited H-Dirksen Bauman, 293–313. Minneapolis: University of Minnesota Press.

Bechter, Frank. 2008. The Deaf Convert Culture and Its Lessons for Deaf Theory. In *Open Your Eyes: Deaf Studies Talking*, edited by H-Dirksen Bauman, 60–82. Minneapolis: University of Minnesota Press.

Benor, Sarah. 2010. Ethnolinguistic Repertoire: Shifting the Analytical Focus in Language and Ethnicity. *Journal of Sociolinguistics* 14(2): 159–83.

Blommaert, Jan, and Ad Backus. 2011. Repertoires Revisited: "Knowing Language" in Superdiversity. Working Papers in Urban Language and Literacies 67. London: Kings College.

Brueggemann, Brenda Jo. 2009. *Deaf Subjects: Between Identities and Places*. New York: New York University Press.

Bucholtz, Mary, and Kira Hall. 2004. Language and Identity. In *A Companion to Linguistic Anthropology,* edited by Alessandro Duranti, 369–94. Malden, MA: Blackwell.

Burghart, Richard. 1984. The Formation of the Concept of the Nation-State in Nepal. *Journal of Asian Studies* 44(1): 101–25.

———. 1993. A Quarrel in the Language Family: Agency and Representations of Speech in Mithila. *Modern Asian Studies* 27(4): 761–804.

Cameron, Mary. 1998. *On the Edge of Auspicious: Gender and Caste in Nepal.* Champaign: University of Illinois Press.

Chomsky, Noam. 1965. *Aspects of the Theory of Syntax.* Cambridge, MA: MIT Press.

Cole, Michael. 1985. The Zone of Proximal Development: Where Culture and Cognition Create Each Other. In *Culture, Communication, and Cognition: Vygotskian Perspectives,* edited by James Wertsch, 146–62. Cambridge: Cambridge University Press.

Curtiss, Susan. 1977. *Genie: A Psycholinguistic Study of a Modern-Day "Wild Child."* Boston: Academic Press.

Daniel, E. Valentine. 1984. *Fluid Signs: Being a Person the Tamil Way.* Berkeley: University of California Press.

De Villiers, Jill, Lynne Bibeau, Elaine Ramos, and Janice Gatty. 1993. Gestural Communication in Oral Deaf Mother-Child Pairs: Language with a Helping Hand? *Applied Psycholinguistics* 14: 319–47.

Devkota, Nirmal Kumar. 2003. Country Paper: Nepal. Paper presented at the Expert Group Meeting and Seminar on an International Convention to Protect and Promote the Rights and Dignity of Persons with Disabilities, June 2–4, 2003, Bangkok, Thailand.

Dirks, Nicholas. 1989. *The Hollow Crown: Ethnohistory of an Indian Kingdom.* Bombay: Orient Longman.

Du Bois, John. 1993. Meaning without Intention: Lessons from Divination. In *Responsibility and Evidence in Oral Discourse,* edited by Judith Irvine and Jane Hill, 48–71. Cambridge: Cambridge University Press.

Dumont, Louis. 1980. *Homo Hierarchicus: The Caste System and Its Implications.* Chicago: University of Chicago Press.

Duranti, Alessandro. 1994. *From Grammar to Politics.* Berkeley: University of California Press.

Eck, Diana. 1982. *Banaras: City of Light.* New York: Knopf.

Emmorey, Karen. 1991. Repetition Priming with Aspect and Agreement Morphology in American Sign Language. *Journal of Psycholinguistic Research* 20: 365–88.

————, and David Corina. 1990. Lexical Recognition in Sign Language: Effects of Phonetic Structure and Morphology. *Perceptual and Motor Skills* 71: 1227–52.

Fisher, William. 2001. *Fluid Boundaries: Forming and Transforming Identity in Nepal.* New York: Colombia University Press.

Fishman, Joshua. 1977. Language and Ethnicity. In *Language, Ethnicity, and Intergroup Relations,* edited by Howard Giles, 15–57. New York: Academic Press.

Friedner, Michele. 2013. Producing "Silent Brewmasters": Deaf Workers and Added Value in India's Coffee Cafés. *Anthropology of Work Review* 34(1): 39–50.

————, and Annelies Kusters. 2014. On the Possibilities and Limits of "DEAF DEAF SAME": Tourism and Empowerment Camps in Adamorobe (Ghana), Bangalore, and Mumbai. *Disability Studies Quarterly* 34(3): 1–22.

Fürer-Haimendorf, Christoph von. 1957. The Interrelations of Caste and Ethnic Groups in Nepal. *Bulletin of the School of Oriental and African Studies* 20: 243–60.

————. 1978. Trans-Himalayan Traders in Transition. In *Himalayan Anthropology: The Indo-Tibetan Interface,* edited by James Fisher, 339–57. The Hague: Mouton.

Gellner, David. 1995. Introduction. In *Contested Hierarchies: A Collaborative Ethnography of Caste among the Newars of the Kathmandu Valley,* edited by David N. Gellner and Decflan Quigley, 1–37. Oxford: Clarendon.

Goldin-Meadow, Susan. 1987. Underlying Redundancy and Its Reduction in a Language Developed without a Language Model: Constraints Imposed by Conventional Linguistic Input. In *Studies in the Acquisition of Anaphora.* Vol. 2, *Applying the Constraints,* edited by Barbara C. Lust, 105–33. Boston: Reidel.

————. 2003. *The Resilience of Language: What Gesture Creation in Deaf Children Can Tell Us about How All Children Learn Language.* New York: Psychology Press.

Goodwin, Charles. 2004. A Competent Speaker Who Can't Speak: The Social Life of Aphasia. *Journal of Linguistic Anthropology* 14(2): 151–70.

Green, Mara. 2014. The Nature of Signs: Nepal's Deaf Society, Local Sign, and the Production of Communicative Sociality. PhD diss., University of California–Berkeley.

Gumperz, John. 1982. *Discourse Strategies.* Cambridge: Cambridge University Press.

————. 1965. Language. *Biennial Review of Anthropology* 4: 84–120.

Guneratne, Arjun. 2002. *Many Tongues, One People: The Making of Tharu Identity in Nepal.* Ithaca, NY: Cornell University Press.

Hakuta, Kenji, Ellen Bialystok, and Edward Wiley. 2003. Critical Evidence: A Test of the Critical-Period Hypothesis for Second-Language Acquisition. *Psychological Science* 14(1): 31–38.

Hangen, Susan. 2005. Boycotting Dasain: History, Memory, and Ethnic Politics in Nepal. *Studies in Nepali History and Society* 10(1): 105–33.

———. 2007. *Creating a "New Nepal": The Ethnic Dimension.* Washington, DC: East-West Center.

Harvey, David. 2005. The Sociological and Geographical Imaginations. *International Journal of Politics, Culture, and Society* 18(3): 211–55.

Haugen, Einar. 1996. Dialect, Language, Nation. *American Anthropologist* 68(4): 922–35.

Hepburn, Sharon. 2002. Touristic Forms of Life in Nepal. *Annals of Tourism Research* 29(3): 611–30.

Hill, Jane. 2008. *The Everyday Language of White Racism.* Malden, MA: Wiley-Blackwell.

His Majesty's Government of Nepal. 1990. *The Constitution of the Kingdom of Nepal 2047 (1990).* Kathmandu: Law Books Management Board.

Höfer, András. 1979. *The Caste Hierarchy and the State in Nepal: A Study of the Muluki Ain of 1854.* Innsbruck: Universitätsverlag Wagner.

Hoffmann-Dilloway, Erika. 2008. Metasemiotic Regimentation in the Standardization of Nepali Sign Language. *Journal of Linguistic Anthropology* 18(2): 192–213.

———. 2009. "Introduction to Linguistic Anthropology." Syllabus. Oberlin College, Oberlin, OH.

———. 2010. Many Names for Mother: The Ethno-Linguistic Politics of Deafness in Nepal. *South Asia: The Journal of South Asian Studies* 33(3): 421–41.

———. 2011a. Lending a Hand: Competence through Cooperation in Nepal's Deaf Associations. *Language in Society* 40(3): 285–306.

———. 2011b. Ordering Burgers, Reordering Relations: Gestural Interactions between Hearing and d/Deaf Nepalis. *Pragmatics* 21(3): 373–91.

Hymes, Dell. 1972. On Communicative Competence. In *Sociolinguistics: Selected Readings,* edited by J. B. Pride and Janet Holmes, 269–93. Harmondsworth: Penguin.

Irvine, Judith. 1989. When Talk Isn't Cheap: Language and Political Economy. *American Ethnologist* 16: 248–67.

———. 2005. Knots and Tears in the Interdiscursive Fabric. *Journal of Linguistic Anthropology* 15(1): 72–80.

———, and Susan Gal. 2000. Language Ideology and Linguistic Differentiation. In *Regimes of Language: Ideologies, Polities, and Identities,* edited by Paul Kroskrity, 35–84. Santa Fe, NM: School of American Research Press.

Jacoby, Sally, and Elinor Ochs. 1995. Co-Construction: An Introduction. *Research on Language and Social Interaction* 28(3): 171–83.

Johnson, Robert, and Carol Erting. 1989. Ethnicity and Socialization in a Classroom for Deaf Children. In *The Sociolinguistics of the Deaf Community*, edited by Ceil Lucas, 41–84. New York: Academic Press.

———, and Elissa Newport. 1989. Critical-Period Effects in Second Language Learning: The Influence of Maturational State on the Acquisition of English as a Second Language. *Cognitive Psychology* 21(1): 60–99.

Joshi, Bikash. 1997. Foreign Aid in Nepal: What Do the Data Show? *Himal South Asia* 10(2): 70–71.

Joshi, Raghav Bir. 1991. Nepal: A Paradise for the Deaf? *Sign Language Studies* 20: 161–68.

Kegl, Judith. 2002. Language Emergence in a Language-Ready Brain: Acquisition Issues. In *Language Acquisition in Signed Languages*, edited by Gary Morgan and Bencie Woll, 207–54. Cambridge: Cambridge University Press.

Kegl, Judith, Ann Senghas, and Marie Coppola. 1999. Creation through Contact: Sign Language Emergence and Sign Language Change in Nicaragua. In *Comparative Grammatical Change: The Intersection of Language Acquisition, Creole Genesis, and Diachronic Syntax*, edited by Michel DeGraff, 179–237. Cambridge, MA: MIT.

Khanal, Upendra. 2013a. Sociolinguistics of Nepali Sign Language with Particular Reference to Regional Variation. BA thesis, University of Central Lancashire and Indira Gandhi National Open University.

———. 2013b. Sociolinguists of Nepali Sign Language in Particular Reference to Age-Related Variation in NSL. Paper presented at SIGN6 conference, February 7–9, 2013, Goa, India.

Kroskrity, Paul. 2004. Language Ideologies. In *A Companion to Linguistic Anthropology*, edited by Alessandro Duranti, 496–517. Oxford: Blackwell.

Lane, Harlan. 2005. Ethnicity, Ethics, and the Deaf-World. *Journal of Deaf Studies and Deaf Education* 10(3): 291–310.

Lane, Harlan, Robert Hoffmeister, and Ben Bahan. 1996. *A Journey into the Deaf-World*. San Diego: DawnSign.

Lave, Jean, and Etiene Wenger. 1991. *Situated Learning: Legitimate Peripheral Participation*. Cambridge: Cambridge University Press.

Lawoti, Mahendra. 2005. *Towards a Democratic Nepal: Inclusive Political Institutions for a Multicultural Society*. Thousand Oaks, CA: Sage.

———. 2013. Transforming Ethnic Politics, Transforming the Nepali Polity: From Peaceful Mobilization to the Rise of Armed Separatist Groups. In *Nationalism and Ethnic Conflict in Nepal: Identities and Mobilization after 1990*, edited by M. Lawoti and S. Hangen, 226–56. London: Routledge.

LeMaster, Barbara, and Leila Monaghan. 2004. Variation in Sign Languages. In *A Companion to Linguistic Anthropology,* edited by Alessandro Duranti, 141–66. Oxford: Blackwell.

Lenneberg, Eric. 1967. *Biological Foundations of Language.* New York: Wiley.

Leontyev, Aleksei. 1981. The Problem of Activity in Psychology. In *The Concept of Activity in Soviet Psychology,* edited by James Wertsch, 37–71. Armonk, NY: Sharpe.

Liechty, Mark. 2001. Consumer Transgressions: Notes on the History of Restaurants and Prostitution in Kathmandu. *Studies in Nepali History and Society* 6(1): 57–101.

———. 2002. Out Here in Kathmandu: Youth and the Contradictions of Modernity in Urban Nepal. In *Everyday Life in South Asia,* edited by D. Mines and S. Lamb, 37–47. Bloomington: Indiana University Press.

———. 2003. *Suitably Modern: Making Middle-Class Culture in a New Consumer Society.* Princeton, NJ: Princeton University Press.

Little, Paul, Alison Bridges, Rajendra Guragain, Del Friedman, Rakesh Prasad, and Neil Weir. 1993. Hearing Impairment and Ear Pathology in Nepal. *Journal of Laryngology and Otology* 107: 395–400.

Maharjan, M., S. Bhandari, I. Singh, and S. C. Mishra. 2006. Prevalence of Otitis Media in School-Going Children in Eastern Nepal. *Kathmandu University Medical Journal* 4(16): 479–82.

Makoni, Sinfree, and Alastair Pennycook. 2007. *Disinventing and Reconstituting Languages.* Bristol: Multilingual Matters.

Mannheim, Bruce. 1999. Iconicity. *Journal of Linguistic Anthropology* 9(1-2): 107–10.

Marriott, McKim. 1959. Interactional and Attributional Theories of Caste Ranking. *Man in India* 39: 92–107.

———. 1976. Hindu Transactions: Diversity without Dualism. In *Transaction and Meaning,* edited by Bruce Kapferer, 109–42. Philadelphia: Institute for the Study of Human Issues.

———, and Ronald B. Inden. 1977. Towards an Ethnosociology of South Asian Caste Systems. In *The New Wind: Changing Identities in South Asia,* edited by Kenneth David, 227–38. The Hague: Mouton.

Mayberry, Rachel, and Ellen Eichen. 1991. The Long-Lasting Advantage of Learning Sign Language in Childhood: Another Look at the Critical Period for Language Acquisition. *Journal of Memory and Language* 30: 486–512.

Mayberry, Rachel, and Susan Fischer. 1989. Looking through Phonological Shape to Lexical Meaning: The Bottleneck of Non-Native Sign Language Processing. *Memory and Cognition* 17(6): 740–54.

McCaskill, Carolyn, Ceil Lucas, Robert Bayley, and Joseph Hill. 2011. *The Hidden Treasure of Black ASL*. Washington, DC: Gallaudet University Press.

Meek, Barbra. 2006. And the Injun Goes "How!": Representations of American Indian English in White Public Space. *Language in Society* 35(1): 93–128.

Milroy, James, and Lesley Milroy. 1999. *Authority in Language: Investigating Standard English*. London: Routledge.

Mines, Mattison. 1994. *Public Faces, Private Voices: Community and Individuality in South India*. Berkeley: University of California Press.

———, and Vijayalakshmi Gourishankar. 1990. Leadership and Individuality in South Asia: The Case of the South Indian Big-Man. *Journal of Asian Studies* 49(4): 761–86.

Mirsha, Chaitanya, and Om Gurung, eds. 2012. *Ethnicity and Federalisation in Nepal*. Kathmandu: Central Department of Sociology and Anthropology, Tribhuvan University.

Mitchell, Ross, and Michael Karchmer. 2004. Chasing the Mythical Ten Percent: Parental Hearing Status of Deaf and Hard of Hearing Students in the United States. *Sign Language Studies* 4(2):138–63.

Monaghan, Leila, Constanze Schmaling, Karen Nakamura, and Graham Turner. 2003. *Many Ways to Be Deaf: International Variation in Deaf Communities*. Washington, DC: Gallaudet University Press.

Morford, Jill. 1996. Insights to Language from the Study of Gesture: A Review of Research on the Gestural Communication of Non-Signing Deaf People. *Language and Communication* 16(2): 165–78.

———, Jenny Singleton, and Susan Goldin-Meadow. 1995. The Genesis of Language: How Much Time Is Needed to Create Arbitrary Symbols in a Sign System? *In Language, Gesture, and Space,* edited by Karen Emmorey and Judy Reilly, 313–32. Hillsdale, NJ: Erlbaum.

Morgan, Michael. 2013. Participant Tracking in Nepali Sign Language Narrative. *Nepalese Linguistics* 28: 86–94.

Narayan, Kirin. 2002. Placing Lives through Stories: Second-Generation South Asian Americans. In *Everyday Life in South Asia,* edited by Diane Mines and Sarah Lamb, 425–39. Bloomington: Indiana University Press.

Nepal National Federation of the Deaf and Hard of Hearing (NFDH). 2003. *Nepāli Sānketik Bhāshāko Shabdakosh (Nepali Sign Language Dictionary)*. Kathmandu: Nepal National Federation of the Deaf and Hard of Hearing.

Neville, Helen. 1995. Developmental Specificity in Neurocognitive Development in Humans. In *The Cognitive Neurosciences,* edited by Michael Gazzaniga, 219–431. Cambridge, MA: MIT Press.

Newport, Elissa. 1990. Maturational Constraints on Language Learning. *Cognitive Science* 14: 11–28.

———, Daphne Bavelier, and Helen Neville. 2001. Critical Thinking about Critical Periods: Perspectives on a Critical Period for Language Acquisition. In *Language, Brain and Cognitive Development,* edited by Emmanual Dupoux, 481–502. Cambridge, MA: MIT Press.

Ochs, Elinor, and Bambi Schieffelin. 1984. Language Acquisition and Socialization: Three Developmental Stories. In *Culture Theory: Mind, Self, and Emotion,* edited by Richard Shweder and Robert LeVine, 276–322. Cambridge: Cambridge University Press.

Ortner, Sherry. 1984. Theory in Anthropology since the Sixties. *Comparative Studies in Society and History* 26(1): 126–66.

Padden, Carol. 1983. Interaction of Morphology and Syntax in American Sign Language. PhD diss., Department of Linguistics, University of California–San Diego.

Pagliai, Valentina. 2011. Unmarked Racializing Discourse, Facework, and Identity in Talk about Immigrants in Italy. *Journal of Linguistic Anthropology* 21(1): 94–112.

Parish, Steven. 1994. *Moral Knowing in a Hindu Sacred City: An Exploration of Mind, Emotion, and Self.* New York: Columbia University Press.

———. 2002. God-Chariots in a Garden of Castes: Hierarchy and Festival in a Hindu City. In *Everyday Life in South Asia,* edited by Diane Mines and Sarah Lamb, 174–89. Bloomington: Indiana University Press.

Pigg, Stacey. 1996. The Credible and the Credulous: The Question of "Villagers' Beliefs" in Nepal. *Cultural Anthropology* 11(2):160–201.

Prasad, Laxmi Narayan. 2003. *Status of People with Disability (People with Different Ability) in Nepal.* Kathmandu: Modern Printing Press.

Raheja, Gloria Goodwin. 1988. *The Poison in the Gift: Ritual, Prestation, and the Dominant Caste in a North Indian Village.* Chicago: University of Chicago Press.

Rai, Janak. 2013. Activism as a Moral Practice: Cultural Politics, Place-Making, and Indigenous Movements in Nepal. PhD diss., University of Michigan.

Rogoff, Barbara. 1990. *Apprenticeship in Thinking: Cognitive Development in Social Context.* New York: Oxford University Press.

Rosaldo, Michelle. 1982. The Things We Do with Words: Ilongot Speech Acts and Speech Act Theory in Philosophy. *Language in Society* 11(2): 203–37.

Rymes, Betsy. 2014. *Communicating beyond Language: Everyday Encounters with Diversity.* New York: Routledge.

Senghas, Richard. 2003. New Ways to Be Deaf in Nicaragua: Changes in Language, Personhood, and Community. In *Many Ways to Be Deaf: International Variation in Deaf Communities,* edited by Leila Monaghan, Constanze

Schmaling, Karen Nakamura, and Graham Turner, 260–82. Washington, DC: Gallaudet University Press.

Sharma, Prayag Raj. 1997. Nation-Building, Multi-Ethnicity, and the Hindu State. In *Nationalism and Ethnicity in a Hindu Kingdom: The Politics of Culture in Contemporary Nepal*, edited by D. Gellner, J. Pfaff-Czarnecka, and J. Whelpton, 471–94. Amsterdam: Harwood.

Sharma, Shilu. 2003. The Origin and Development of Nepali Sign Language. MA thesis, Tribhuvan University, Kathmandu.

Sharmacharya, Dipawali. 2000. Recollection of a Journey. *Bahirā Āwāj* (*Voice of Deaf*), 9–12. Kathmandu: The National Association of Deaf and Hard of Hearing Nepal.

Shneiderman, Sara. 2013. Developing a Culture of Marginality: Nepal's Current Classificatory Moment. *Focaal: Journal of Global and Historical Anthropology* 65: 42–55.

———. 2014. Reframing Ethnicity: Academic Tropes, Recognition beyond Politics, and Ritualized Action between Nepal and India. *American Anthropologist* 116(2): 279–95.

———, and Mark Turin. 2006. Revisiting Ethnography, Recognizing a Forgotten People: The Thangmi of Nepal and India. *Studies in Nepali History and Society* 11(1): 97–181.

Shweder, Richard, and Edmund Bourne. 1984. Does the Concept of the Person Vary Cross-Culturally? In *Culture Theory*, edited by Richard Shweder and Robert LeVine, 158–99. Cambridge: Cambridge University Press.

Sidnell, Jack, and Nick Enfield. 2012. Language Diversity and Social Action: A Third Locus of Linguistic Relativity. *Current Anthropology* 53(3): 302–21.

Silverstein, Michael. 1976. Shifters, Linguistic Categories, and Cultural Description. In *Meaning and Anthropology*, edited by Keith Basso and Henry Selby, 11–55. New York: Harper and Row.

———. 1979. Language Structure and Linguistic Ideology. In *The Elements: A Parasession on Linguistic Units and Levels*, edited by R. Cline, W. Hanks, and C. Hofbauer, 193–247. Chicago: Chicago Linguistic Society.

———. 1996. Monoglot "Standard" in America: Standardization and the Metaphors of Linguistic Hegemony. In *The Matrix of Language: Contemporary Linguistic Anthropology*, edited by Donald Brenneis and Ronald K. S. Macaulay, 284–306. Boulder, CO: Westview.

Skinner, Debra, and Dorothy Holland. 1996. Schools and the Cultural Production of the Educated Person in a Nepalese Hill Community. In *The Cultural Production of the Educated Person*, edited by Bradley Levinson, Douglas Foley, and Dorothy Holland, 273–300. Albany: State University of New York Press.

Spitulnik, Debra. 1996. The Social Circulation of Media Discourse and the Mediation of Communities. *Journal of Linguistic Anthropology* 6(2): 161–87.

Srinivas, Mysore Narasimhachar. 1967. Cohesive Role of Sanskritization. In *Unity and Diversity: India and Ceylon,* edited by Philip Mason, 67–82. London: Oxford University Press.

Stokoe, William. 1960. *Sign Language Structure.* Silver Spring, MD: Linstok.

Tamang, Mukhta Singh. 2009. Tamang Activists, History, and Territorial Consciousness. In *Ethnic Activism and Civil Society in South Asia,* edited by David N. Gellner, 269–90. New Delhi: Sage.

Taylor, Irene. 1997. *Buddhas in Disguise: Deaf People in Nepal.* San Diego: DawnSign.

Tedlock, Dennis, and Bruce Mannheim. 1995. *The Dialogic Emergence of Culture.* Chicago: University of Illinois Press.

Tetreault, Chantal. Forthcoming. Ethnographic Perspectives on Panel Studies and Longitudinal Research. In *Using Panel Data in the Sociolinguistic Study of Variation and Change,* edited by Suzanne Wagner and Isabelle Buchstaller. Routledge Studies in Language Change Series. Routledge Press.

Urban, Greg, and Benjamin Lee, eds. 1989. *Semiotics, Self, and Society.* Berlin: Mouton de Gruyter.

Volosinov, Valentin. 1973. *Marxism and the Philosophy of Language.* Translated by Ladislav Matejka and I. R. Titunik. New York: Seminar.

Vygotsky, Lev. 1978. *Mind in Society: The Development of Higher Psychological Processes.* Cambridge, MA: Harvard University Press.

Wiesel, Torsten, and David Hubel. 1963. Effects of Visual Deprivation on Morphology and Physiology of Cells in the Cat's Lateral Geniculate Body. *Journal of Neurophysiology* 26(6): 978–93.

Wilce, James. 1998. *Eloquence in Trouble: The Poetics and Politics of Complaint in Rural Bangladesh.* Oxford: Oxford University Press.

Wrigley, Owen. 1996. *The Politics of Deafness.* Washington, DC: Gallaudet University Press.

Zeshan, Ulrike. 2000. *Sign Language in Indo-Pakistan: A Description of a Signed Language.* Philadelphia: Benjamins.

Index

Figures and notes are indicated by f *and* n *following the page number.*